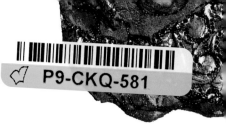

Paper, Metal, and Stitch

Creating Surfaces
with Color and Texture

Paper, Metal, and Stitch

Creating Surfaces
with Color and Texture

Maggie Grey and Jane Wild

 INTERWEAVE PRESS

Acknowledgments

We would like to thank our families for all their support, our friends for lending work, and Michael Wicks for wonderful photography. Finally, we would like to remember Jane's mum Prue, and Louise.

First published in 2004 by

B T Batsford
Chrysalis Books Group
The Chrysalis Building
Bramley Road
London W10 6SP
www.batsford.com

Volume © B T Batsford
Text and drawings © Maggie Grey and Jane Wild 2004
Photography by Michael Wicks (© B T Batsford)

First edition for North America published in 2005 by Interweave Press, Inc.

All inquiries should be addressed to:
Interweave Press, Inc.
201 East Fourth Street
Loveland, CO 80537 USA
www.interweave.com

Printed by Times Offset, Malaysia for the publishers

Library of Congress Cataloging-in-Publication Data

Grey, Maggie, 1947-
  Paper, metal, and stitch : creating surfaces with color and texture /
Maggie Grey and Jane Wild.
    p. cm.
  Includes bibliographical references and index.
  ISBN 1-931499-97-7
  1. Embroidery, Machine. 2. Mixed media textiles. I. Wild, Jane. II. Title.
  TT772.G74 2005
  746--dc22

                                    2005000084

10 9 8 7 6 5 4 3 2 1

Frontispiece
Ancient Emblems: 12 x 8 in (3 x 20 cm). A background of tea-dyed calico was built up with distressed Lokta paper and embossed metal shim. The metal was colored with patination fluids and antiqued with black acrylic paint. Borders were made from stitched gold kid and metal shim with Lazertran transfers applied.

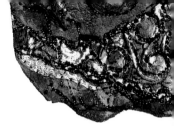

Contents

Introduction

Mixed media textiles are becoming very popular—increasingly so as stitchers see the wonderful results that can be obtained by using paper and metal in their work. Paper can be molded, formed, cut, torn, and stitched, and the techniques used in this book will enable large- or small-scale projects to be tackled with confidence. Metal adds a seductive gleam and new dimensions are explored using fine, soft, sheet metals, meshes, wires, and coils.

This book will be of interest to all who work in the craft field. In it, we aim to lead the reader through the basic first steps to exciting ideas for combining techniques and using both paper and metal in new ways with a variety of media.

The materials used range from tomato purée tubes to brown paper, and very little special equipment is needed. Most will be found in your workroom—or kitchen!

You'll find lots of new ideas and innovative methods, from melting techniques for embossing powders to using paper with heat-reactive threads.

Using the book

The book is divided into two parts—Paper and Metal. The two parts follow a similar pattern, describing forming methods, ways of adding color and texture and, finally, stitch. They are presented in a logical manner, enabling you to follow them through or to dip in and out as the fancy takes you. Most of the ideas can be intermixed and can be combined, bringing together paper and metal. Approach all the ideas with an open mind. Be willing to experiment and you will make many additional discoveries.

The methods described (for paper-making by Jane Wild, and for metal by Maggie Grey) work for us but are by no means the only approaches. Adapt them, extend them—and you'll not only find new ways but have a lot of fun.

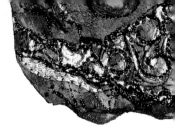

Part One: Paper

1
Paper Textures

Paper is a natural material made from plant fiber. It is freely available and inexpensive. We use it every day, often without a second thought. Yet it is such a versatile medium and full of creative potential. Paper can be manipulated or molded into any shape or form and assume any surface quality, it can be used successfully on a large or small scale, it may appear strong and sturdy or quite fragile. Machine-made and handmade papers provide a rich source of alternative surfaces for a variety of stitch techniques. Paper can also be used to enhance and embellish stitched items and, by experimenting with the following techniques, unique and exciting work can be created.

Purchased papers

Many unusual and exotic papers such as Lokta, Kozo, and Japanese lace paper are available from art, craft, or specialist paper suppliers. These papers are often chosen for their unusual appearance or for particular surface qualities and, as many of them are surprisingly strong, they can withstand quite rough treatment. They are ideal to use as surfaces for stitch. Everyday papers such as brown (Kraft) paper, water-color paper, and tissue, are also full of potential and can be transformed with quite simple treatments.

A selection of purchased papers including Japanese lace paper, gold wrapping paper, and Lokta paper embedded with skeleton leaves.

Opposite: Cas Holmes' *After the Rain* (detail) 80 x 32 in. (200 x 160 cm) This piece contains blueprint fabric, layered papers, emulsion transfer, dye paste, and stitch, and is the artist's own technique. Inspired by the issues of flooding, it conveys how the beauty of water can hide hard truths about our perceptions of environmental conditions.

Using an incense stick to burn holes in some Japanese lace paper.

Cutting, tearing, and burning

By cutting, tearing, or burning paper, you can create different edges: Soft, hard, wispy, or ragged. Experiment with the following ideas, compare the results and see how they work together. Sometimes the contrast of a cut edge against a torn or burned one can be quite dramatic.

Paper has a grain and tears more easily in one direction. To see the difference, take a sheet of paper and tear a strip from side to side, then from top to bottom. The same applies if the paper is folded first and then torn along the fold, or torn against the edge of a ruler. Try this and the following suggestions with a variety of papers.

- Tear some paper toward you then away from you and see how the edges differ. The effect is more pronounced when one side of the paper is a different color or printed.
- Cut paper with as many different tools as you can, for example knives, pinking shears, nail or decorative scissors, or cut shapes with craft or stationery punches.
- Cut a shape (circle or square) in paper and then cut it into segments. Now tear the same shape and then tear that into segments. Arrange both shapes on a contrasting piece of paper and note the differences in character.
- Vary the manner in which you cut or tear: Quickly, slowly, roughly. Try to control the paper or allow it to influence the outcome.
- Use a brush loaded with water to draw a line or shape on a piece of paper. Allow the water to soak into the fibers and then gently tear along the line. This method is useful if the paper is difficult to tear or you want more control over tearing.
- Hold a lighted incense stick against the edge of a piece of paper and, when it starts to smolder, blow gently to control the burning. Press the burning tip of the incense stick against the paper to burn holes.

Any burning should be managed safely. Work outside or in a well-ventilated room and have a container of water on hand.

Top: Cut and torn shapes were arranged on a strip of brown paper and applied by hand and machine. Below: Paper strips cut and torn to produce a variety of edges.

Opposite: An incense stick was used to burn edges and holes in various exotic papers. Gold leaf and inks were applied to some before they were burned.

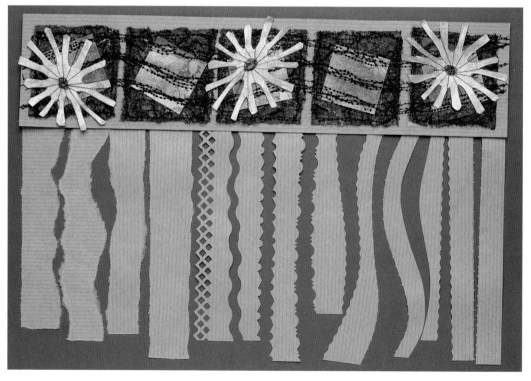

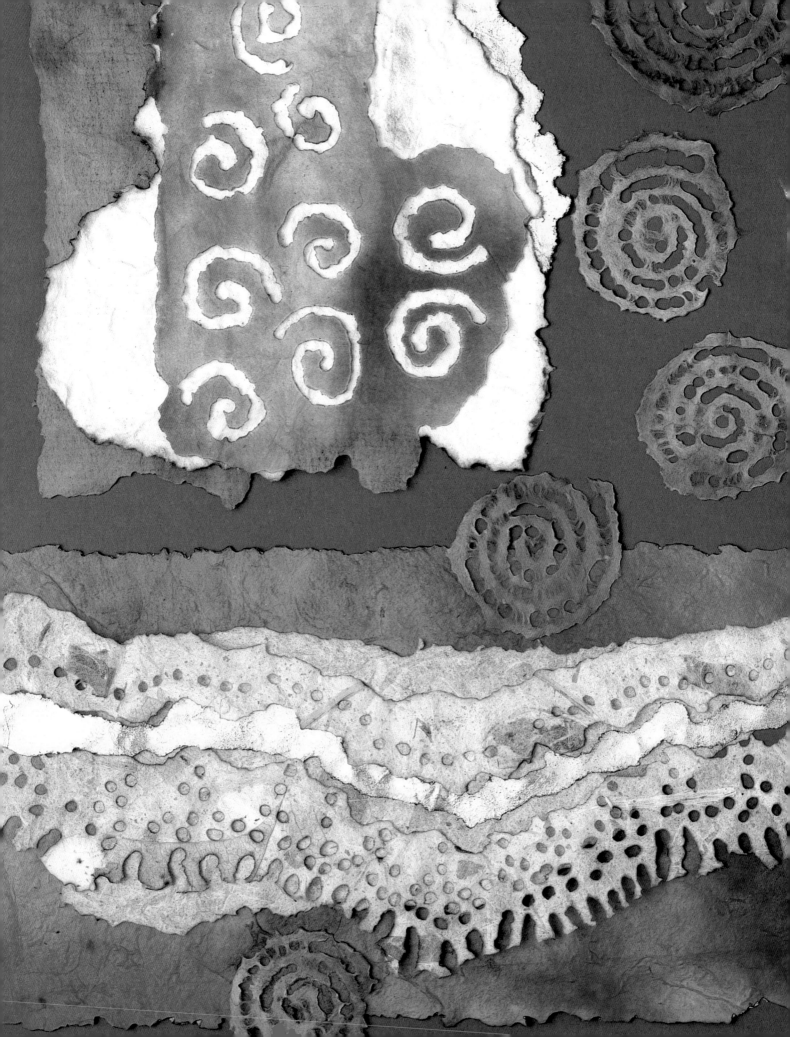

Crumpling and creasing paper

Simply crumpling or creasing a sheet of paper creates many surface patterns and textures. Repeatedly crumpling and creasing paper also softens the fibers, making it easier to stitch. Papers respond differently to crumpling. Some soften and others form hard creases, or tear. Experiment with as many papers as you can. Wet some paper before crumpling it and then manipulate it into a pleasing arrangement of folds and creases. Leave to dry and you will have a surface crying out for stitches, beads, or other forms of embellishment.

Create a ruched effect by wrapping and crumpling paper around a plastic tube or plastic ruler. Place a piece of Lokta or another long-fiber paper in a bowl of water. Gently wring out and then wrap it loosely around a plastic tube. Scrunch the paper down gently but firmly to gather it up. Let it dry out completely—this may take a day or so—then carefully unwind the paper. It may feel as though it's stuck but just pull it slowly and steadily and it will unwind. Vary the effect with the following.

- Try other papers. Some may be more difficult to scrunch down and might need to be tied with string to prevent them unraveling.
- Vary the way you scrunch the paper.
- Try painting the paper with ink or dye before it dries.

Soak a piece of Lokta or Kozo in water, squeeze to remove excess water, gently crumple and then place on a waterproof surface. Dip your finger or a brush in some water and make small circular movements on the paper. This will distress the surface causing thin areas or holes and ridges to form. You can create highly textural and lacy effects and also manipulate or mold the paper while it's wet. You can also crumple a piece of damp Kozo repeatedly until it starts to weaken then pull, gently teasing out the fibers. Some bits will break off with soft wispy edges.

Ruching Paper

1. Damp paper rolled loosely around a plastic tube.

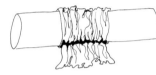

2. Paper firmly scrunched.

3. Unrolling the paper when it's dry.

4. A variation, paper scrunched in places.

The arrows in this diagram represent the circular and rolling movements used to distress a piece of Lokta.

Ruched brown
paper and natural
Lokta overlaid with
colored, ruched
Lokta and a piece
of distressed Kozo.

Piercing paper

Paper can be pierced with almost any pointed instrument, and variations in the scale and density of the holes produced will create many different effects. Brown (Kraft) paper is a good first choice, but try other papers as well and experiment with the following.

- Place a sheet of paper, right side down, on a thick, soft pad of felt or blanket, and pierce with various pointed instruments. Enlarge some holes by pushing a pencil through—this is particularly effective with painted or printed paper.
- Layer three or four pieces of paper on a soft pad and pierce the entire area fairly evenly with the point of a small skewer or a large needle. Concentrate the piercing in certain areas until the paper starts to tear and break up, then crumple and rub the layers together to encourage the distress. The layers can be applied to a backing as they are, or separated and used individually or to build up an area of texture.
- Try heavy piercing in straight lines, curves, or isolated shapes for different effects.

Ideas for piercing paper.

- You can also use a sewing machine with an unthreaded needle to "stitch" grids or random patterns. The machine can be set up for normal stitching or for free-form stitching, whichever you prefer, and several layers can be stitched at one time. When the stitching is complete, remove the paper and separate any layers then crumple and distress until you are happy with the result. You could also scorch the edges with an incense stick.

Above: this piece of bark was the inspiration for several experiments with pierced paper.

Experimental bark piece: 11 x 6 in. (29 x 15 cm). Four layers of brown (Kraft) paper, pierced, distressed, and torn were free-form machine stitched to a paper backing. Highlights were added with gilding wax and various threads were twisted, wrapped with enameled wire, and couched into position.

Etched paper

Paper-Etch Dissolving Gel is a product that creates some exciting effects by carving into the surface of paper. It works by attacking cellulose fibers when heat is applied. The most dramatically carved effects are seen on very thick watercolor paper but, when used on less substantial paper, you can etch right through it. Paper-Etch can be applied straight from the bottle, used with a stencil, brushed or stamped on, but don't use a wooden print block as the gel will attack the wood.

Below left: Paper-Etch experiments on various papers including a tea bag and paper decorated with ink.

Start with heavyweight smooth-surfaced watercolor paper. Rinse it under the tap for a minute or so to remove some of the size. When the paper is dry, draw a simple shape with Paper-Etch straight from the bottle, using varying amounts, and then put aside to dry. Place on a heat-resistant surface and zap with a heat tool, or cover with baking parchment and iron (don't use steam) until the treated area turns brown. Hold the paper under running water while you remove the brown area with a soft brush. When the paper is dry, you could apply more Paper-Etch to increase the effect. Also try the following.

Below right: Paper-Etch applied to paper (top); after heating with a heat tool (middle); scorched areas were removed and the surface inked to show the effect (bottom).

- Experiment with other papers. Remember that Paper-Etch will eat right through some papers, so make sure your designs or shapes will remain attached to the paper (think of stencil designs).
- Try it on the back of paper painted with acrylic paint—it removes the paper but not the paint.
- Paint the paper with watercolor paint, ink, or very diluted acrylic paint before applying Paper-Etch.

Acrylic texture gels and gesso

There are many acrylic gels available containing added materials for creating different surface textures. These can be mixed with acrylic paint or painted at a later stage. By varying the method of application, many different effects can be achieved. The textures really come to life when painted and highlighted. Some texture gels may be too tough to stitch into, so you may wish to mask the areas to be stitched.

See how many effects you can create by applying texture gels or gesso with brushes, palette knives, rollers (brayers), sponges, and print blocks—then experiment further.

- Make your own texture gels by adding different materials such as sand, sawdust, or beads, to an acrylic medium or PVA.
- Use the gel or gesso as an adhesive and adhere items to the surface.
- Apply a layer of texture gel or acrylic gesso and work into the surface with various mark-making tools. Paint the surface and, when dry, twist the paper and distress it until the paper tears in places. Then place the paper right-side down and brush with ink. It should seep into the cracks and creases.

Experimental samples, all painted with burnt umber acrylic and highlighted with gilding wax. Specific effects include: Crushed sea shells in gesso, and scrim embedded in gesso. Pebeo mica mortar, garnet gel and gold mica medium (Golden products) were also used.

Puff paint

Puff paint colored with a tiny amount of black acrylic paint then rubbed with gilding wax after heating. The samples include puff paint applied with a roller then overprinted with a spiral print block and sprinkled with tiny beads (left), applied irregularly with card stock (top), and applied with a palette knife and drawn into with a shaper tool (below).

Puff paint is a binder that expands when heated. Subtle or flamboyant effects can be achieved depending on the method of application and the quantity used. It can be colored before application with a little acrylic paint or colored with various media after heating. Apply the puff paint, then place on a heat-resistant surface and heat with a heat tool, taking care not to scorch it. Remove the puff paint from brushes and rollers with water immediately after use.

Apply puff paint using a variety of tools, such as rollers, print blocks, or card stock, and vary the quantity used. Perhaps drop small beads or glitter into it before heating.

Making your own paper

So far we have achieved some exciting results with purchased papers. However making your own paper is very satisfying and having an experimental approach to the process opens up many creative possibilities. The techniques we shall use do not require perfectly made paper—often less than perfect results and "mistakes" have a special quality that can be quite inspirational. Japanese papermakers believe that every sheet of handmade paper reflects the qualities of the maker. We shall look at papermaking in sufficient detail for the purposes of this book, but should you wish to experiment further, there are several excellent books available to borrow from a library or to buy (for details see Resources on page 126). Most of the materials and equipment required for papermaking are easy to obtain and inexpensive or can be adapted from everyday items.

Materials and equipment

Pulp: Cotton linters are part-processed cotton fibers in sheet form and are readily available from many art and craft suppliers. We shall assume they are used to make pulp. Other fibers can be used and the techniques will still work but the results may be different.

Bowl or bucket: You will need a waterproof container to soak the linters, and a sieve to strain the pulp.

Mold and deckle: The mold is a mesh-covered frame used to scoop up pulp from the vat. The deckle is an empty frame that sits on top of the mold and helps to keep the pulp in place and shape the edges of the paper. They are available in different sizes and can be obtained from various suppliers (see Resources, page 126). An embroidery hoop can be used as an alternative. The Anchor Flexi-Hoop and Picture Frame works well. Varnish the frame if it is wooden, stretch some mesh (such as net curtaining) taut in the frame, trim back the excess and it is ready to use. An empty hoop can be used as a deckle.

Aluminum mesh: Use a fine mesh of the sort used to repair car bodywork. It can be cut to the required size and shape and used without the support of a frame.

Blender: A domestic blender is used to beat the pre-soaked cotton linters to form the pulp.

Vat: This holds the pulp suspended in water. Any plastic container large enough to take the mold and deckle comfortably will do.

Felts: Wet-formed paper is transferred to a cloth or "felt." Use disposable kitchen cloths or interfacing.

Pressing boards: You will need these to remove excess water from wet-formed paper. Any waterproof boards can be used.

Newspaper and old towels: Have a good supply on hand for mopping up. Papermaking is a very wet occupation!

Basic papermaking

1   Soak a small quantity of cotton linters in water for a few hours or overnight. Tear into small pieces, about 1 in. (2.5 cm) square and place a small handful in the blender. Half-fill with water and operate in short bursts of about 15 to 20 seconds, resting between bursts. Five or six times should be sufficient to break down the linters. The pulp should be lump free and feel silky when ready.

2   Pay attention to your blender. Don't allow it to overheat. If the motor seems to be laboring, turn it off, remove some of the pulp and add a bit more water. You will get to know what suits your machine. Just proceed cautiously.

3   Half-fill the vat with water, warm or cold, and add some pulp, about one part pulp to four parts water. The consistency should be similar to pancake batter.

4   A couching (pronounced "KOO-ching") mound makes it easier to transfer wet-formed paper from the mold. You can build one while the pulp is settling. Fold newspapers into small, medium, and large rectangles and place them on top of each other starting with the smallest. Place a felt on top and moisten before use.

5   Stir the mixture in the vat to distribute the pulp, and hold the mold (and deckle) vertically over the vat. Then, in one continuous movement, lower the mold halfway into the vat, move it to a horizontal position and bring it up steadily, allowing the water to drain away for a few seconds. Gently agitate the mold to settle the fibers and remove the deckle if you are using one.

6   Hold the mold in front of you, with the pulp facing up. Then turn the mold 90 degrees and place the right-hand side of the mold onto the left-hand side of the mound (pulp facing the mound). Roll the mold onto the mound, press down then

roll off again. The sheet of wet-formed paper should be on the felt and the mold resting on its left-hand side. Cover with a felt and form the next sheet on top and continue in this way, adding more pulp to the vat as necessary. If at any stage you're unhappy with the results, float the pulp back into the vat and try again. To make thicker paper, either increase the quantity of pulp in the vat or layer two or more sheets of wet-formed paper.

7 To remove excess water, place some newspaper on the floor, then sandwich four to six sheets of wet-formed paper, interleaved with felts, between the pressing boards and stand on top of them. After pressing, leave the paper on the felt and hang it on a line to dry, or experiment with a bit of texture. When the paper is dry, it can be peeled off the felt.

Don't pour any pulp down the sink or drain; always strain the water from the vat before disposing of it.

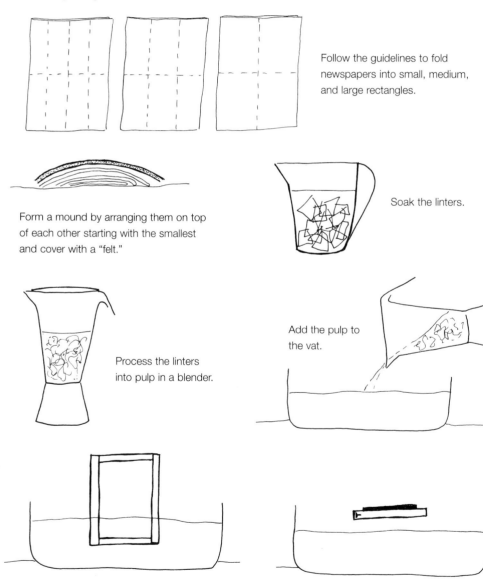

Follow the guidelines to fold newspapers into small, medium, and large rectangles.

Form a mound by arranging them on top of each other starting with the smallest and cover with a "felt."

Soak the linters.

Process the linters into pulp in a blender.

Add the pulp to the vat.

Dip the mold into the vat.

Scoop out some pulp on the mold.

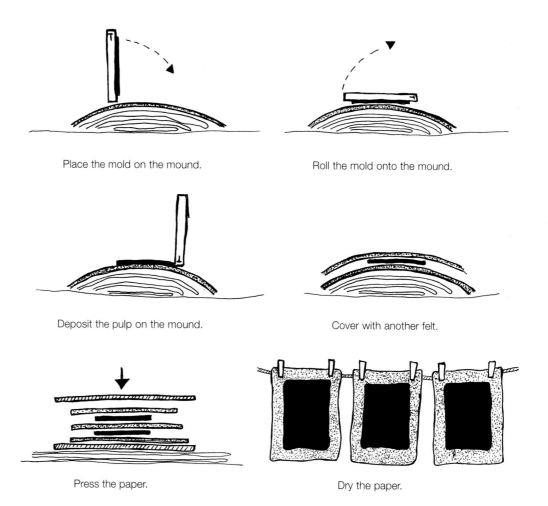

Place the mold on the mound.

Roll the mold onto the mound.

Deposit the pulp on the mound.

Cover with another felt.

Press the paper.

Dry the paper.

Texturing paper

Texture can be created and decorative elements added at various stages in the papermaking process. One of the simplest methods is to place a thick sheet of unpressed wet-formed paper (on a felt) on the mold or a piece of mesh, and drip or spray water onto the surface to make holes and craters. Allow the water to drain away and then hang to dry. Try the same technique with a stencil or another form of mask.

Textured molds for sheet-forming

The texture of a sheet of paper is partly determined by the mesh on which it is formed. A closely woven mesh produces a uniform sheet of paper. Experiment with different openweave fabrics and lace by stretching them in an embroidery hoop (see page 20) and using those as a mold. You can also use materials such as plastic mesh, a lacy plastic table covering and bamboo table mats as alternative molds without having to stretch them in a frame. These will all produce papers with different textures. You can form the sheet in the usual way but you may not be able to couch (transfer) it onto the mound—in which case leave it on the mold to dry then carefully peel it away.

Dip different items—wire shapes, skeleton leaves, or lace—into the vat and they will get a covering of pulp.

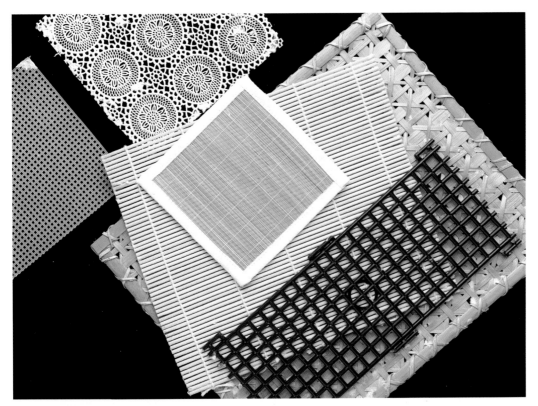

A selection of materials used as alternative molds.

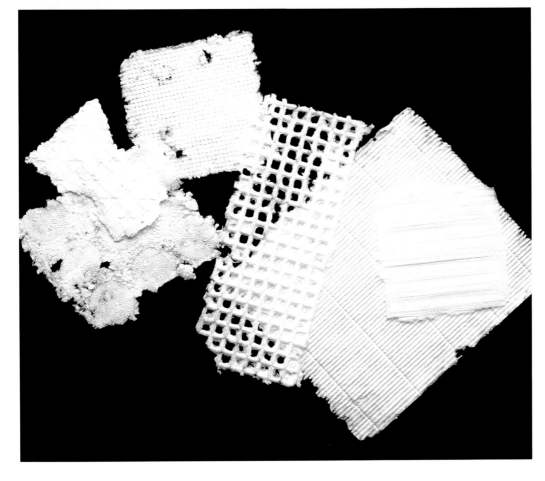

Textured paper formed on alternative molds.

Embossing

We use the term embossing in this book to describe various techniques, including the use of embossing powders to produce relief designs on paper or metal.

Paper is embossed by impressing it with interesting objects or textured surfaces. Objects with well-defined surfaces and edges will produce the most accurate impressions but it is worth trying anything that appeals, for example leaves, grasses, shells, lace, stencils—the possibilities are endless. Use thick paper for embossing to prevent the object from tearing the surface—unless, of course, you fancy a distressed piece. Have plenty of pulp in the vat, make several sheets of thick paper and press them lightly. Leave the paper on the felt, place the objects on the paper and cover with another felt. If the objects are not too fragile, sandwich everything between two boards and stand on them or press firmly with your hands. Remove the objects and allow the paper to dry.

Try the following variations.

- Use a selection of objects such as kitchen utensils, tools, springs, or keys to texture the surface. Vary the way you impress the surface. Try pressing, pressing and twisting, hitting, or rolling the objects.
- Make shapes from wire or foamboard to emboss with and cover with a textured fabric rather than a felt, before pressing.
- Try embossing with textured and patterned rollers or print blocks. Indian wooden print blocks quite often stain the paper, which adds to the effect.

A selection of tools used for embossing paper and the resulting paper.

Embedded paper

When paper is embedded with decorative and textural material, the material is held in place by the fibers of the pulp, creating interesting effects and changing the surface quality of the paper. Snippets of thread or fabric, *potpourri*, beads, sequins, or seeds can be added to the vat. The resulting paper will contain these additions and every sheet formed will be unique. Another way of embedding additional material is to sandwich it between two sheets of wet-formed paper and then press the sheets together. You have more control over the position and quantity of material with this method, as the following suggestions illustrate.

- Experiment with different materials. For example, embedding wire or Wireform would enable you to bend and shape the paper.
- Embed various fabrics to reinforce the paper for stitch.
- Tear back part of the top sheet to reveal some of the embedded material.
- Try combining the techniques. For example, embed some paper with cheesecloth, emboss it, and then manipulate into ridges and pleats.

A detail from *Whispers* (page 51). Embedded Wireform in the pulp has created a strong and flexible surface.

2

Paper Shaping

Variations using the collagraph mold (see page 32). Left: Heavy lace was torn and placed on the mold and pulp pressed on top to form a fragment. Middle: The mold was lined with Lokta tissue, the design free-form machine stitched onto cold water-soluble film and placed on the tissue. Wet-formed paper was pressed firmly on top. Right: Fragment cast using pulp mixed with snippets of metallic fabrics then painted with gesso.

Paper can be used with a variety of molds. Using molds for paper casting and *papier mâché* techniques enables basic structures or units to be repeated. As these can be varied at the molding stage, it is possible to produce related rather than identical pieces. These can then undergo similar or different treatments, be integrated into one piece of work or form a series. The molded paper is just the beginning.

Ready-made molds for various crafts and baking purposes can be used, or you can make your own, which is fun and often produces unexpected results. Molds can be built from scratch or taken from a master shape. Several materials and methods can be used, each with its own characteristics. Decorative frames or moldings, found items, and print blocks can be used as alternative molds. The resulting shaped paper will be a negative impression of the original.

Making molds

Polymer clay and Softsculpt (Formafoam) are versatile materials and simple or complex molds can be made easily and fairly quickly. Both materials can be impressed and manipulated. The impressions can be used in a variety of ways: As individual molds to produce small items for embellishment, or several impressions can be combined to form more complex molds. Have a selection of objects to impress with, such as interesting buttons, jewelry, print blocks, molding mats, shells, fossils, lace, and ornaments.

Polymer clay

Condition the clay well, either by rolling it in your hands or passing it through a pasta machine (which should not then be used for cooking) until it is soft and pliable. Roll out the clay—the size and thickness will depend on the object to be impressed. Dust both sides of the clay with cornstarch or talc to prevent it sticking to the mold or to your fingers. Press the object into the clay. If you want to increase the depth of the mold, gently push up the edges. Remove the object carefully, place the clay on a metal tray and bake according to the manufacturer's instructions. Then try the following variations.

- Roll out some polymer clay, cut or tear it into fragments, and make random impressions from the same object. These can be rejoined or baked separately.
- Remove the object from the clay and then distort the impression slightly before baking.
- Take and bake an impression from a print block, tile, or similar object. Then take an impression from this. Bake it and you have positive and negative molds to use.

Above: A molding mat and polymer clay impressions.

Below: Paper cast using the molding mat and clay impressions. Background paper is decorated with Shiva (Markal) rubbings taken from molding mat.

Softsculpt (Formafoam)

Softsculpt is thermoplastic foam available in thick and thin sheets; thick sheets are better suited to mold-making. It can be heated in an electric oven, with a heat tool or an iron, then quickly shaped around or impressed with an object. The results are not always predictable, but this adds to the appeal. If you're unhappy with any shape or impression, simply reheat and Softsculpt returns to its flat state. It retains heat for only a matter of seconds so it is important to have everything you require on hand. Cut some Softsculpt to size and heat, following the manufacturer's instructions, and then experiment with the following (note that there will be a difference in the depth and accuracy of the impressions).

- Place an object on a firm surface, quickly cover with heated Softsculpt, and press firmly with your hand until the impression is made.
- Repeat with another piece of Softsculpt but, this time, use a board to press down with.
- Another effect can be achieved by placing the object on a slightly textured surface.
- Place a piece of heated Softsculpt on a firm surface and impress with an object, then repeat with another piece of Softsculpt on a padded surface.

Left: A Softsculpt (Formafoam) impression made with a button.
Top: A paper cast adhered to some epoxy putty (to add weight) and decorated with acrylic paint and Pearl Ex powders.
Right: Pendants featuring similar paper casts combined with beads.

Fixing several related impressions to a firm sealed surface such as Medium Density Fiberboard (MDF) or plywood can make an interesting mold resembling a print block. Cut your chosen surface to the required size and arrange the impressions on it. Try several arrangements. Different effects will be achieved by butting the impressions together or spacing them apart. Remember that the mold is negative, so everything is in reverse. A gap between impressions will produce a ridge in cast paper. To fix the impressions to the background, apply PVA glue to both surfaces and leave for a few minutes until tacky. Arrange the impressions, cover with a board and clamp it in place. Leave for a few hours or overnight.

Left: A complex Softsculpt (Formafoam) mold made with impressions taken from a small clay head and a chess piece from a casting kit. The resulting cast was created using wet-formed paper.

Below left: A mold for casting a frame, the raised section in the center produces a recess.
Below middle: A frame cast, using wet-formed paper, was painted with gold acrylic then Liming wax (a Liberon product) applied and partially removed with clear wax. The recess can be seen in this example.
Below right: Pulp containing snippets of fabric was used to cast a fragmented frame. Burnt umber acrylic was diluted and allowed to trickle over a base of acrylic interference colors. Impressed pulp forms the insert.

Quite complex molds can be built using this technique. By alternating textured, patterned and plain areas or varying the depth of the Softsculpt components, it is possible to create molds designed to frame or provide areas to incorporate stitched or mixed media pieces.

Making a Softsculpt vessel:

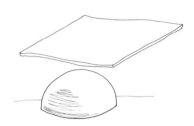

1. Mold heated Softsculpt (Formafoam) around a small vessel.

2. Make several impressions and cut them out.

3. Cut holes in the Softsculpt using the impressions as a guide.

4. Fix the impressions in place with PVA.

To make three-dimensional molds with Softsculpt, choose simply shaped objects that you can encompass easily with both hands. For example, to make a mold for a vessel, select a suitable object, cut a piece of Softsculpt large enough to cover it, heat in the oven and place over the object, wrap your hands around it and press. Remove the Softsculpt from the object. The edges will be fairly ragged but these can be trimmed back to give a neat edge, or you may like to leave some of the folds and creases and just snip into parts of the edge.

Once you have a three-dimensional mold it is possible to insert small pieces of impressed Softsculpt. Remember that you are working in reverse, so the impressed shape will produce a raised effect on the finished item. Place the impressed Softsculpt face down on the outside of the mold and carefully cut around it. Remove the cut-out, then brush the edges of the hole and the impressed Softsculpt with a little PVA glue. Leave for a few minutes until the glue is tacky and then insert the impressed Softsculpt and press into place. It will probably not be a particularly neat fit but, as long as it is secure, it will hold up during use.

When you have made and used a three-dimensional mold, it is easier to see the potential in different objects. For example, try molding around a ball of string or some fabric that has been twisted and wrapped with knotted threads. Alternatively, look at the various seed pods and other botanical products available from florist and craft suppliers.

Far left: A piece of Friendly Plastic was heated and impressed then embedded in a solvent-free adhesive like No More Nails to form a small low-relief mold.
Center: A latex mold was made.
Left: By using both molds, positive and negative paper casts were made.

Collagraph method

The plates used for collagraph prints are made by gluing a variety of textural materials to heavy-duty card stock. We can adapt this technique to produce low- to high-relief molds, on surfaces such as medium-density fiberboard (MDF), plywood, or suitable objects such as plates, bowls, and frames. You may already have made a collagraph plate, in which case thoroughly seal all sides with varnish before using it as a mold.

Opposite: A vessel was cast in three-dimensional Softsculpt. (Formafoam) mold, covered with gold leaf, and painted with black spirit-soluble dye then sponged with denatured alcohol.

Making a collagraph

Before you start, consider the following.

The cast paper will be a negative impression of the mold, so a mirror image of any design should be transferred to the MDF. If you want to create a raised area in the cast, it must be recessed in the mold and vice versa.

Don't create undercut areas when building up or carving into a surface. Keep the edges straight in a U shape or a V shape, otherwise paper may get pushed under the surface of the mold and tear when you remove it.

U-shaped and V-shaped grooves in cross section.

Make sure that everything is sealed with two or more coats of waterproof varnish, to prevent water seeping in and spoiling the mold.

- Start with a small piece of MDF or plywood and have a selection of interesting materials at hand, for example card, textured papers and fabrics, string, or skeleton leaves. Use PVA or an acrylic medium as an adhesive and build up a low relief pattern or design with some of your materials. Leave for 24 hours or until the adhesive is dry and then seal with varnish.
- Or, cover your surface (MDF) with a thick layer of acrylic modeling paste or home improvement adhesive or caulk. Build up a design by drawing into the paste with any mark-making tools, impressing the surface or embedding items. When satisfied with your design, leave it to set. This may take a few days if the paste is thick. Seal with varnish.

Undercut grooves in cross section: paper will get trapped and may tear.

• Tear different sizes of strips and shapes from thick blotting paper, coat them generously with acrylic gel medium and start to layer them onto your chosen surface. Work intuitively, building up interesting shapes and patterns or follow a simple design. As the gel soaks in, the blotting paper becomes quite soft and you can work into the surface with a stick or similar tool for details. When set, seal with varnish.

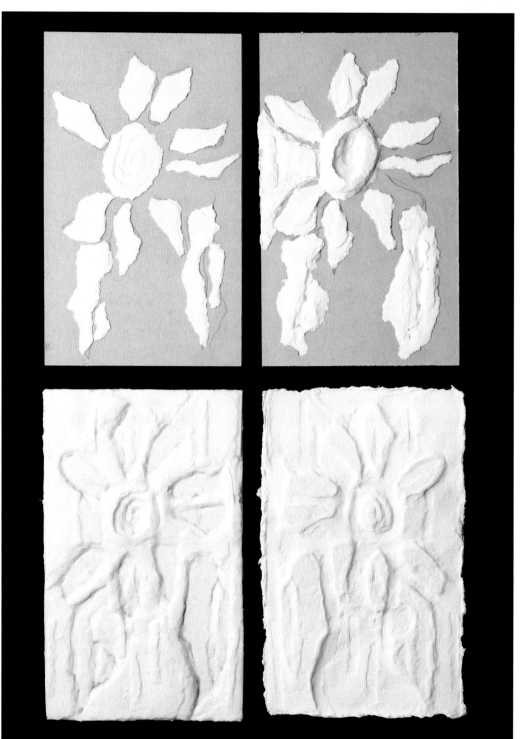

Making a collagraph mold. Top left: The design drawn and the main areas defined with torn blotting paper. Top right: Building up the background. Below left: The mold, finished and sealed. Below right: The resulting paper cast, the recessed areas of the mold produce the raised areas in the cast.

Making a master shape

Master shapes or forms can be modeled in media such as clay, polymer clay, and plasticine, or constructed with any materials that can be shaped and fixed into the desired form. Flexible or rigid molds can be taken from the master and it can also be used as a mold for *papier mâché* techniques.

For example, the master for a vessel can be constructed from corrugated paper cut to the height of the vessel plus roughly 2 in (5 cm), rolled to the diameter of the base and taped securely. More corrugated paper can be added to the roll to form a basic structure, which can be refined by adding a combination of paper and various acrylic gels, heavy body medium, or gesso. A form constructed in this way will have to be completed in stages to allow time for the acrylic gels to harden. Texture and relief patterns can be added to the surface by applying papers, fabric, found items, texture gels, or dimensional paints. Seal with two or three coats of varnish.

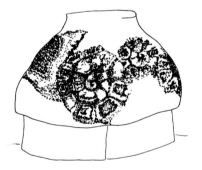

1. Basic shape formed with rolled corrugated card.

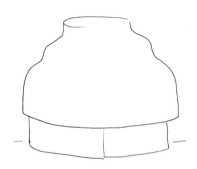

2. Shape refined with paper and acrylic modeling paste.

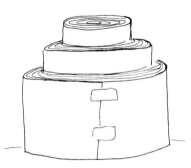

3. Torn photocopies arranged as a basis for a relief design.

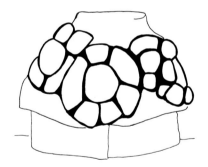

4. Design shapes simplified and built up with blotting paper and acrylic heavy gel medium.

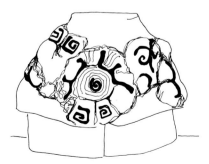

5. Texture created with tissue paper and heavy gel medium and detail added with relief outliner.

Latex rubber

Latex liquid rubber is an emulsion that air-dries on the surface of a master shape and forms a rubber skin that is extremely flexible. Two mold-making techniques can be used, dipping and paint on.

Dipping is the best method for masters made from porous materials such as plaster of Paris, fired clay, or wood. Generally speaking, the master is dipped into the latex for a few seconds, removed and any air bubbles burst, then re-dipped for 15–20 minutes, removed and left to cure overnight. To prevent sticking, dust the mold with talc before peeling it from the master.

For masters made from non-porous materials, the paint-on method is better. Several layers are painted on with a soft brush, being allowed to part-cure between applications. As many as 8 to 15 layers may be needed depending on the size of the master. Cheesecloth can be sandwiched between the layers to strengthen the mold. Cure and release as above.

Opposite: A cameo (top) was used to make the Mold 'n' Pour mold (right). The casts were made with wet-formed paper and one (below) was covered with gold leaf and painted with brown spirit-soluble dye and denatured alcohol.

Below: A fragmented vessel was cast with pulp containing snippets of fabric using the latex mold (in the background beside the master form). The vessel was decorated with faux verdigris (page 45). Copper wax and turquoise paint were used and "knocked back" with black patinating wax.

Mold 'n' Pour

A product called Mold 'n' Pour is ideal for making small, flexible molds. The pack contains a blue and a white compound. Knead equal quantities of these until the colors blend, then place on a flat surface and impress with an object. Wait for about ten minutes, then remove the object and the mold is ready to use.

Alternative molds

Print blocks, especially some of the large ones, can be used as molds, and interesting effects can be achieved by combining printing and casting from the same print block. Positive and negative aspects of design can be explored. Other objects can be used as paper casting and *papier mâché* molds: plastic packaging, basketwork, stones, stone moldings, decorative wrought iron, and trees.

Using the Molds

Paper casting

Compressing pulp or wet-formed paper into a mold forms a paper cast. Both methods produce a cast with good detail, although surface quality differs. A cast made using the pulp method has a slight additional texture to it. Paper shrinks as it dries so it is better to cast around the inside surfaces of an object or mold to prevent cracking. Paper should release easily from flexible molds or those with a shiny surface but, if in doubt, use petroleum jelly or silicon spray as a release agent.

The same mold was used to make casts from wet-formed paper (left) and pulp (right); both casts were painted with burnt umber and bronze acrylic.

Pulp method

Select a mold or object to cast from and apply a release agent if necessary. Prepare enough pulp to make the cast. This will probably be more than you expect, so have plenty available. Take a small quantity of strained pulp and place it in the mold. Press it lightly with a sponge to remove some of the excess water. Continue in this way until the pulp covers the mold and is at least 1/2 in (12 mm) thick. Then press the pulp firmly with a sponge to compress it and remove as much water as possible. Leave to dry—this may take some days, depending on the size and thickness of the cast and atmospheric conditions.

Adding cellulose paste powder or PVA to the pulp will strengthen the cast, but it will make it tougher to stitch. Dissolve 1 tablespoon (15 ml) of cellulose paste powder in a small amount of water, or dilute the same quantity of PVA in a little water and mix with the pulp. These quantities are a guide only and can be varied.

Making a paper cast by pressing pulp into a mold.

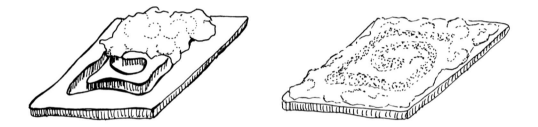

Wet-formed paper method

Make several sheets of wet-formed paper as described on page 20 and lightly press them. Prepare a mold by applying a release agent, if necessary.

Carefully tear one of the wet sheets into manageable pieces and place one of these against the mold. Use a brush or sponge to work it into the mold. Continue in this way, overlapping the edges for a seamless finish. Vary the position of the edges when placing the second and subsequent layers to prevent ridges forming. Use a sponge to compress the cast and remove excess water when all the layers are in position. The cast can be reinforced with a coat of cellulose paste between each layer. A cast of between two and six layers will be quite strong, but not too difficult to stitch into.

As with the pulp method, the cast may take some days to dry. Paper shrinks as it dries so it may pucker slightly. If you don't want this to happen, place a weight or another means of restraint on the paper while it dries.

Making a paper cast with wet-formed paper, freshly made and lightly pressed.

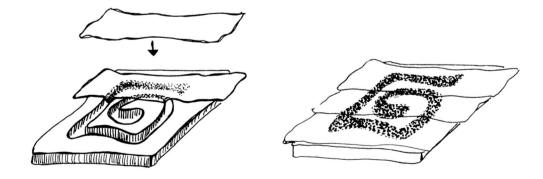

When you're familiar with both methods, try the following variations.

- Cast a portion of the mold, or vary the thickness of pulp, so that the cast is uneven or fragmented.
- Tear and arrange wet-formed paper irregularly in the mold.
- Dip a piece of cheesecloth in cellulose paste and then sandwich it between layers of wet-formed paper to strengthen the cast. Alternatively, cast sections of the mold so that some of the cheesecloth is visible.
- Try the techniques with different types of pulp or mix different pulps together and see how the results vary.
- Add snippets of fabric and lace, or other textural elements, to the pulp. Add a little PVA before casting with it.
- Place some torn lace, beadwork, or *potpourri* into the mold, then cast using either method. When dry, apply a coat of acrylic varnish or PVA glue.
- When a vessel, frame, or surface has been cast, inserts or additional sections can be made. Protect the surface with plastic wrap and then build up the insert or section with pulp. Leave to dry.

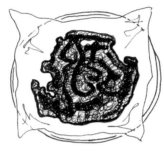

1. The vessel lined with plastic wrap.

2. The insert formed with pulp.

3. The finished insert that can be painted, then stitched or beaded.

Below left: A vessel decorated using the faux verdigris technique (see page 45) in oxidized gold wax and purple acrylic.
Below right: An insert for the vessel. Pieces of chiffon scarf were attached to the insert with beads and a heat tool used to distress the chiffon.

Papier mâché

Torn strips of paper are layered and bonded over a mold or support to form *papier mâché* items. Use Mulberry tissue, Lokta, or other long-fiber papers to make quite distinctive *papier mâché*.

Apply a layer of petroleum jelly to the mold as a release agent and prepare the adhesive: One part PVA mixed with one part water. Tear the paper into small 1–2 in (2–5 cm) squares or strips. Position the paper on the mold and work in the adhesive with a brush. Continue until there are about ten layers. Leave to dry and then remove the *papier mâché* from the mold. It may be necessary to cut it to aid removal. If so, use PVA to bond the edges and layer more paper over the join.

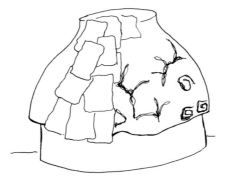

Using the master as a mold for a *papier mâché* vessel.

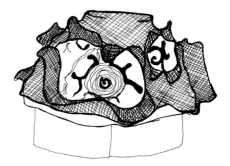

Wireform three-dimensional shape formed over the master.

Alternatively, you can shape Wireform into a three-dimensional structure and cover both sides with *papier mâché*, wet-formed paper, or a combination of both.

The techniques explored in this and the previous chapter can be combined, so experiment freely. The worst that can happen is that some materials may be wasted, but you will gain more experience of the medium and its potential. Keep asking "What if. . . ?"—and see where it takes you.

Torn and molded Wireform covered with Mulberry tissue was used as the basis for a vessel. Cast paper inserts were added and the vessel decorated using the faux verdigris technique (see page 45) in a combination of copper wax, purple and turquoise acrylic, and black patinating wax. The early stages of a similar vessel can be seen in the background.

3

Color and Metal Effects on Paper

White paper allows form and texture to be appreciated without distraction, but color can enrich, make a statement, or create a mood. Many techniques can be employed to add color and metal effects to machine- or hand-made paper or paper objects. It is always worth spending time building up an effect as it will have more depth and interest, but remember to keep a note of the media used and the order of application since you may wish to duplicate it.

A selection of painted papers. Brushes and sponges were used to apply acrylic paints in various combinations.

Surface decoration

Sealing the surface

Handmade paper should be sealed before applying any surface treatments, for protection and to provide a stable ground to work on. Several products can be used. Apply one or two coats of PVA diluted half-and-half with water as a general sealant. Acrylic gesso provides a more substantial seal. Apply at least two coats and remember that you can add texture at this stage by sponging, impressing, or by adding texture gels once the gesso is dry. Acrylic paint can also be used. The first coat will sink into the paper slightly, and a second coat will be necessary. Some combinations of sealant and surface decoration will make the paper quite tough to stitch (though rarely impossible) and this may determine when you stitch.

Metallic and distressed surfaces

The appeal of metal objects lies in the uneven texture, color, and patina they display, so it's a good idea to look at the real thing, then create realistic effects or let your imagination run wild as you wish. Metal effects are achieved with real metal or colored mica (pearl or luster) powders and both are available as raw materials or in a range of media: paint, oil bars, pastels, transfer foil, or leaf.

Paint

Acrylic paints are particularly versatile. They are available in a wide range of intermixable colors including metallics. They can be used to cover any porous surface and will dry quickly. Remember to wash acrylic paint from brushes, as dried-on paint is difficult and sometimes impossible to remove.

Building up layers of color often results in a richer effect than mixing the same colors together and applying them as one color. Try the following suggestions and then see how many variations you can come up with.

- Apply paint with various tools. Experiment with different consistencies of paint and combine texture gels with paint.
- Sponge or paint the surface with acrylic paint. Add a different color to some acrylic glaze medium and sponge or paint over the first color. Glaze medium extends the working time of the paint, so you can texture or remove some of the glaze by sponging or stamping into it. You can use artist's quality paints and glazes.

Texture was added to a paper cast by attaching a chiffon scarf to the surface with Wonder Under, or other fusible webbing, and zapping it with a heat tool. The surface was sealed and reactive bronze paint applied. Several coats of the blue patina topcoat were allowed to trickle over the paint. The surface was enhanced with burned lace paper and painted stitch.

Paper casts made using large foam print blocks and a Softsculpt mold. Top: Copper and black were sprayed heavily from opposite directions over a burnt umber base. Middle: Copper and gold were sprayed heavily over a base of burnt umber. Black patinating wax was worked into some areas. Bottom: Copper and pearly blue were sprayed from opposite directions over a black base.

- Experiment with different combinations of more than one base color or glaze. Try metallic and interference colors as a base or a glaze.
- Start with a textured and painted base, work a layer of colored glaze into it and wipe over the surface with a cloth before the glaze dries.
- Think of other ways to apply glazes: print or stencil, drag or scrape them on; work them into the detail; or use a dry brush with a little glaze and flick it over the surface.
- Seal a textured paper surface, or create a textured surface with gesso. Dilute one or more acrylic paints with water and apply randomly to the surface. Spray with water to move the paint around, then allow to dry. The pigment will collect unevenly on the surface.

Some paints are designed for use with embossing powders and can be safely heated. The Stewart Gill range of acrylic paints is an example. Apply a thick layer of paint to a paper surface, place the paper on a heat-resistant surface immediately and zap it with a heat tool. The paint will bubble up to form a crusty surface.

There are several paint systems that include reactive metal paints. These are made with real metal particles and, when treated with aging solutions, verdigris and rusted metal effects can be created. Paint and aging solutions can be brushed, sponged, or sprayed on for various realistic effects.

You could also try the aging solutions with other metallic media: spray paint, or gilding wax. If there is metal content, it may patinate.

Metallic spray paint can be used to create some striking effects. Experiment with the following.

- Spray a base coat and, before the paint has dried, spray with other colors.
- Spray a dark textured surface from one direction and then spray with another color from the opposite direction.
- Lightly spray some textured handmade paper with metallic spray paint and/or highlight with gilding wax. Dip it in a dyebath, allow the dye to soak in, carefully remove it and place on a plastic surface to dry.

Bronze and luster powders

Bronze powders are finely ground metal particles available in several shades of gold, copper, silver, and some metallic colors. Luster or pearl powders are made from mica and, unlike bronze powders, are non-toxic and will not tarnish. Luster powders are available in a wide range of metallic and interference colors. Experiment with the following to see the variety of effects you can achieve.

- Make your own paint or glaze by adding either type of powder to any acrylic medium, gum arabic, or shellac. Gradually add the powder to the binder and mix it thoroughly.
- You can also add the powders to paint—keep testing the mixture until you have the right effect.
- Try brushing bronze or luster powders over a tacky surface such as PVA, acrylic size, or paint before it has dried. The powder will adhere.
- Melt some beeswax in a waxpot/melting pot, or in a small container in a pan of boiling water. Do not allow the wax to overheat. Use tweezers and dip a piece of paper into the hot wax, transfer the paper to a heat-resistant surface covered with

baking parchment and then re-melt the wax with a heat tool. Sprinkle with bronze or luster powder before the wax sets. Re-melt the wax again and allow the bronze powder to move around. You could also impress the wax with a seal or decorative metal button.

Wear a respirator or mask, work in a well-ventilated area and wash your hands after using these materials. Always add the powder to the binder and use a damp brush to transfer the powder to a tacky surface.

Metal leaf

Metal leaf is available loose or on a carrier sheet (transfer leaf), in gold, silver, and copper or as an imitation gold and silver. Some manufacturers supply different-colored flakes of metal leaf for random application. Pure gold will not tarnish but other metal leaf will. If you want to prevent this or halt any patination effect, then protect with a coat of shellac. Transfer leaf is ideal if the surface is flat or highlights are required, but three-dimensional and relief items should be covered with loose leaf.

A selection of cast, woven, crumpled, and ruched papers dipped in melted wax and decorated with bronze and Pearl Ex powders. Some have also been sprinkled with glitter and tiny beads.

Apply a coat of acrylic size to a sealed paper surface and leave for 15 minutes or until tacky. For transfer leaf, lay the sheet on the surface and rub firmly with your finger. Lift the sheet and the leaf should have adhered to the size.

Applying loose leaf is also fairly straightforward. Size the surface as before, dust your hands with talc, and very carefully pick up a piece of metal leaf. Drape the leaf over the surface and use a brush to work it into the surface. Overlap with another piece of leaf and brush this into place. Continue in this way, covering any gaps with more leaf. Dust the surface with a soft brush to remove any flaky bits.

A Softsculpt (Formafoam) mold was impressed with shaped copper wire and used to make several paper casts. Metal leaf was applied to the casts and we experimented with some of the ideas described on the opposite page.

Opposite: faux verdigris samples.
From the top:
1. Burnt umber acrylic paint, gold wax, shellac.
2. Gold wax, periwinkle and navy blue paint/denatured alcohol, gold highlights.
3. Gold wax, plum and orange paint/denatured alcohol, lighter gold highlights.
4. Ruby wax, periwinkle, orange and turquoise paint/denatured alcohol, gold highlights.
5. Oxidized gold wax, turquoise paint/denatured alcohol, oxidized gold highlights.
6. As Sample Two with black patinating wax applied.
7. Silver wax, navy blue paint/denatured alcohol, ruby highlights.

Further ideas

- Cover a paper item with copper leaf, place on a heat-resistant surface and zap with a heat tool until the color starts to change. Stop heating when you're happy with the color.
- Apply metal leaf flakes to some parts of a sized surface and then brush the remaining area with glitter and/or metal and luster powders.
- Experiment with patinating fluids and household cleaning products such as bleach and ammonia. Apply a little at a time to judge the effect, then rinse with water.
- Rub the surface with wire wool to distress or remove parts of the metal leaf.

Gilding wax

Gilding waxes such as Treasure Gold/Jewels or the Liberon range are available in a number of metallic colors and can be used to cover large areas or to highlight. Apply gilding wax with a brush, a cloth or your finger and work it well into the surface. It can be left matt or buffed to a soft sheen after 24 hours. Try the following variations.

- Apply one or more gilding waxes to a sealed, textured surface and follow this with a layer of black patinating wax (a Liberon product). After a few minutes, use a cloth to remove as much of the excess as you wish. Add highlights with gilding wax.
- Combine other non-metallic white or colored waxes with gilding waxes to produce some interesting effects.
- Brush some areas of a gilded surface with luster powders to enrich the color.
- To make faux verdigris, apply one or more gilding waxes to a sealed, textured surface and, while the wax dries, mix one part acrylic paint (liquid craft color) with six to ten parts denatured alcohol (DA). Paint the waxed surface with shellac or french polish and wait until it is touch dry—a few minutes usually. Hold the textured surface vertically and stir the paint/DA mix. Load a brush and press it against the top. The mix should trickle down. If not, add more DA until it does. As the paint and DA do not mix properly and the DA attacks the shellac or french polish, a patinated effect is achieved. After a few hours, highlight some areas with gilding wax.

Spirit-soluble dyes

Spirit-soluble dyes are available in intermixable colors and can be combined with denatured alcohol (DA) on a metallic surface for some exciting effects.

Denatured alcohol is ethyl alcohol that has been altered to render it poisonous to drink; never use it near children. Methanol (or methylated spirits), also poisonous and flammable, is often hard to find in the United States but may be used instead. When combining DA with spirit-soluble dyes, wear a respirator and rubber gloves and work in a well-ventilated room or outdoors. Spirit-soluble dyes are highly flammable, harmful if inhaled, and can irritate the skin and eyes.

Cover a paper surface with metallic paint, metal leaf, or gilding wax. Load a soft brush with spirit dye and paint the surface with one or more colors. Pour a small quantity of DA into a glass jar, dip a brush or cotton bud into the jar, and drip or brush the DA onto the surface. Watch the reaction between the DA and the dyes. Use an oil-based varnish to seal the surface.

Try different methods for applying DA: stencils, sponges, rollers, or rubber stamps. Alternatively, for a different effect, dilute the dyes with DA before applying them.

Transfer foil

A range of metallic and holographic effects that can be transferred to almost any surface are available on plastic carrier sheets. Apply PVA or acrylic size to a paper surface and wait for it to become tacky. Cover the area with a piece of transfer foil, shiny side up, and rub

Top: A cast paper book cover: 11 x 5 in (28 x 13 cm), covered with variegated metal leaf, painted with orange and brown spirit-soluble dyes and worked into with denatured alcohol (DA). Below: Samples of spirit-soluble dyes and DA on paper covered with imitation gold leaf. Below right: A piece of impressed Softsculpt (Formafoam) was used to print onto an area of metal leaf painted with spirit soluble dye and then printed off onto an unpainted area.

firmly with your finger to transfer the effect. If it doesn't transfer, cover with parchment paper and press lightly with a cool iron. Transfer foil is particularly effective when used to add highlights. Large areas of uniform application tend to look a bit obvious. Alternatively, try the following.

- Bond some cut or torn Wonder Under (fusible webbing) to a decorated paper surface, remove the backing paper, and place a piece of transfer foil on top. Cover with parchment paper and use the tip of a cool iron to press the foil lightly. Lift the foil regularly to monitor progress.
- Apply acrylic paint to a textured surface, leave to dry then brush the raised areas with acrylic size (two coats may be necessary). When the size is tacky, transfer some holographic foil and then brush the entire surface with spirit dye or spirit-based glass paint.

Embossing powders

Embossing powders are available in a wide range of colors including metallics and when melted with a heat tool they form a raised surface. They must be adhered to the surface before heating, otherwise the heat tool will blow the powder away. Apply embossing fluid or paint with a brush, roller (brayer), sponge, or rubber stamp and sprinkle the surface with powder. Tap to remove the excess powder, then place on a heat-resistant surface and melt with a heat tool. Some unusual effects can be created with embossing powders.

- Remove some Wonder Under (fusible webbing) from its backing, tear into small pieces and place on a paper surface. Carefully melt it with a heat tool. The Wonder Under will shrivel, so keep adding more until you're happy with the effect. Sprinkle with embossing powder, remove the excess, then melt the powder and sprinkle with more powder before it cools, then melt that as well. You can also sprinkle with tiny beads or mica flakes before it sets.
- Cut or tear a square of Wonder Under and bond it to a paper surface with an iron. Remove the backing paper, zap the Wonder Under with a heat tool and sprinkle with embossing powder.
- Apply a thick layer of paint from the Stewart Gill range or similar pigments, sprinkle some areas with embossing powder, then zap with a heat tool.
- Ink up a rubber stamp or a piece of impressed Softsculpt, then build up two or three layers of embossing powder. Before the final layer sets, impress it with the stamp. When it has cooled, remove the stamp.

Below left: Torn Wonder Under (fusible webbing) and two coats of embossing powder were applied to plain and cast papers and the surface brushed with ink. Below right: Ink and a mixture of embossing powders were applied to three paper tiles; Softsculpt (Formafoam) was inked and then used to impress two of the tiles. A paper fragment was pressed into the embossed surface of the other tile before it cooled.

Combining techniques

Four stages showing the development of decorated brown paper; the materials are listed in order of use.
Left: Shiva (Markal) paintstick and black ink. Wonder Under, colored with metallic paint and ironed. Embossing powder. More embossing powder and black ink.
Middle: Metallic and glitter wax crayon, black and brown ink. Painted Wonder Under, zapped with a heat tool. Embossing powder. More embossing powder, gilding wax and Pearl Ex.
Right: Glitter wax crayons and blue ink. Colored Wonder Under, ironed. Another layer of Wonder Under, ironed and worked into with Shiva paintsticks. Zapped with a heat tool and rubbed with gilding wax.

Thoroughly crumple a piece of brown paper, scribble on it randomly with metallic oil or wax crayons, and then brush with ink. Leave to dry. Peel the backing from some painted or unpainted Wonder Under (fusible webbing) and drape it over the paper. Zap with a heat tool or cover with baking parchment and hover an iron over the top to melt the webbing onto the paper without flattening it. Sprinkle some embossing powder onto the melted webbing and heat. Apply transfer foil or work into the surface with metallic Shiva (Markal) paintsticks or try a combination. Brush with more ink or paint and keep going until you're happy with the effect.

Color some Japanese lace paper with metallic Shiva paintsticks and leave for about 48 hours to dry. Tear about four pieces roughly the same size, layer and stick them together with diluted PVA then manipulate into a pleasing shape and leave to dry. Or tear the lace paper into small pieces and use to make a *papier mâché* object. You can use a small butane-fueled blowtorch (the type used in the kitchen) to scorch and distress the paper. Work outside over a bowl of water, light the blowtorch and hold the paper with pliers. Gently play the flame over the surface. It will start to buckle and scorch. By allowing the paper to ignite then blowing out the flame repeatedly, you can slowly burn holes and edges. Drop the paper in the water if you're unable to extinguish the flame.

Draw a pattern or design on paper with PVA glue and allow to dry. Paint the surface with colored ink (not acrylic) or watercolor paint. Brush some areas with Pebeo Mica Mortar when the ink has dried and then follow with a coat of black ink (not acrylic). Use a brush or sponge to apply a little household bleach, diluted with water, to lighten and texture some areas. The final touch is to add highlights with transfer foil. Breathe on the PVA to activate it, place the foil shiny side up on the glue and rub, adding a little at a time.

Japanese lace papers, colored with metallic Shiva paintsticks, layered and molded, then scorched with a domestic blow torch. Molds include a large foam print block (top middle) and a mask-making mold.

A design: 20 x 14 in (52 x 34 cm), worked in PVA glue and decorated with inks, Pebeo mica mortar, bleach, and transfer foil.

4

Into Paper with Stitch

As we have seen, paper is an exciting and versatile medium. Many shapes and surfaces can be created and materials such as fabric, metal, and plastic can be combined successfully with paper or paper objects. Stitch can be added in a variety of ways. It may be functional, forming part of the structure, linking both visually and physically, or finishing edges. It may also be used to enhance by adding texture, pattern and color or to secure other items.

Time Passes: 36 x 15 in (90 x 38 cm). In this delightfully distressed work, calligrapher Elizabeth Forrest has covered string and knots with paper pulp. This enhances the calligraphy on smooth, handmade paper.

Approach stitch flexibly. Consider simple stitches as a means of mark making, stitching before painting and decorating the surface, embedding stitch in the paper as you make it, or experimenting with a favorite technique to see if it can be adapted.

We use the term patch in both parts of the book to describe any shaped piece of paper or metal that is applied to another surface. In most cases, the patches are constructed, stitched, or decorated prior to application.

Reinforcing paper for stitch

Paper doesn't have to be reinforced but using a stabilizer or backing will strengthen it, help prevent stitches pulling through or tearing the surface, and add weight to fragile or lightweight papers. Reinforce paper with a stabilizer such as iron-on interfacing, which is available in several weights and easily applied. Alternatively, use Wonder Under (fusible webbing) to bond paper to various materials. Bonded paper can look flattened but this can be overcome by crumpling the paper before bonding, not applying too much pressure with the iron, or crumpling and distressing it after bonding. An alternative is simply to back the paper with felt or sew-in interfacing without bonding it in place.

Select one type of paper and experiment with different backings, interfacing, fabric, or metal shim to see how the handle of the paper is affected.

You can also strengthen paper as you make it by sandwiching fabric or Wireform between sheets of wet-formed paper.

Papers such as Japanese lace paper can be strengthened with a coat of acrylic varnish without clogging up the holes, so the paper can be caught down using up and down stab stitches. Lay the paper on baking parchment or waxed paper and brush on the varnish, using the matt finish unless you want shiny paper.

Whispers: 7 x 6 in (18 x 17 cm), areas of a Softsculpt (Formafoam) mold were covered with layers of wet-formed paper. Torn Wireform was dipped in the vat for a covering of pulp, placed on the mold, and more pulp pressed on top. When dry, the Wireform was flexed to lift parts of the cast. A few handstitches were added and gesso applied followed by a coat of blue acrylic, and finally gold acrylic and burnt umber glaze.

Stitching by hand

Simple stitches can be used to great effect, adding emphasis rather than overwhelming paper surfaces. The best way to explore the combination of paper and stitch is to work a few samplers using a variety of threads and paper surfaces. To begin with, experiment with stitches such as straight, running, chain, cross, buttonhole, and fly. Vary the size and style of the stitch: Regular, irregular, or loose. Apply gesso, texture gel, and emulsion or acrylic paint to one of your samplers, including the stitches. Then highlight some areas of stitch with gilding wax.

Cut or tear several paper patches, varying the size but keeping to the same shape. Then apply them to a paper background by stitching around the edges, through the shapes or by holding them in place with a single stitch.

Hand stitches

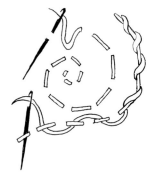

Straight stitch

Running and whipped running stitch

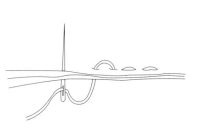

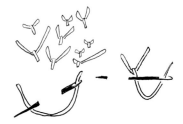

Stab-stitch

Cross-stitch

Buttonhole stitch

Chain and detached chain

Fly stitch

Applied stitch

Stitching into a paper surface is not always practical. It may be too tough or you may want the stitch element to be visible from one side only. In either case, another ground can be stitched and then applied to the surface with an acrylic medium or PVA. Almost any fabric can be used, adding texture and stitch to the surface and then painted or not, depending on the desired effect.

Stitching with the machine

With the machine set for normal stitching (feed dogs up) and some of the paper reinforced with interfacing (sew-in or iron-on), try the following.

- Stitch a series of lines in straight stitch or zigzag, or use built-in stitch patterns if you have them. Vary the size of the stitch and the distance between the stitches. Crumple the paper first and see if that makes a difference.
- Tear or cut a patch and apply it to a piece of paper, using one of the stitches from your experiments.
- Use the built-in stitch patterns to stitch strips or shapes on paper (without a support), then tear along the stitches to form braids and patches.

Set the machine for free-form stitching by fitting an embroidery foot, dropping the feed dogs, and adjusting the thread tension if necessary. In general, paper won't need to be framed for free-form machine stitching. Select a piece of reinforced paper and stitch straight or curving lines to get the feel of it. Stitch at a comfortable speed and avoid jerky movements. If you overstitch an area, the paper will tear.

From a selection of decorated papers, tear or cut patches in different sizes and shapes and arrange them on a larger piece of reinforced paper. A tiny spot of PVA will hold them in place.

Left: Decorated papers wrapped with chenille.

Middle: A piece of woven paper dipped in wax and covered with bronze powder was attached to the background with one large detached chain stitch. Detached chain was also used to attach small paper patches decorated with gold leaf and spirit-soluble dye.

Right: Various papers were layered in this sample, including construction paper decorated with gesso and gold acrylic then distressed and inked. Running stitch was used to apply and link the paper elements.

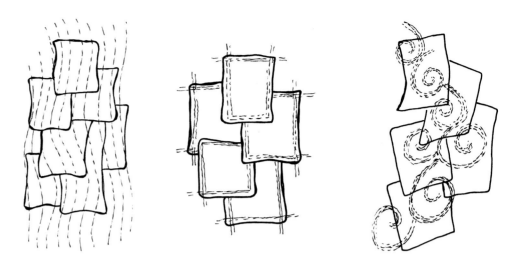

Ideas for applying patches by machine.

There are several options now. The shapes can be outlined or blended into the background with stitch or secured with stitched lines, patterns, or motifs.

Softsculpt (Formafoam) impressed with a lace flower was used to cast several fragments. The fragments were colored with gilding wax and ink then free-form machine stitched to paper backgrounds.

When applying cast paper fragments to another surface, you may want to blend the edges. This can be achieved with dense free-form machine stitching between the fragment and the surface, although it may distress the fragment. Another method is to cover the fragment and part of the surface with a loosely woven fabric, manipulate the weave until most of the fragment is visible (but the edges are all or partly obscured) then free-form machine stitch to blend. A mixture of hand and machine stitch is another option.

Links

Hand-stitched links

Link separate units or fragments of paper/cast paper with variations of lacing or insertion stitches. The fragments or units are likely to have uneven edges and surfaces, so allow the pieces to sit comfortably, adjusting the distance between the edges and the stitch tension as you work. Piercing holes in the edge prior to stitching can make the process easier, particularly if you are working with unwieldy pieces.

Cretan insertion

Buttonhole insertion

Lacing

Chain worked over lacing

Raised chain band

Needle weaving

Three cast paper fragments, formed on a Softsculpt (Formafoam) mold, were linked with insertion stitches and embellished with needle weaving, bullion stitches, and beads.

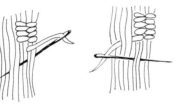

Link papers to form a book .

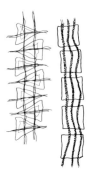

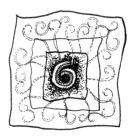

Link small patches to form orders.

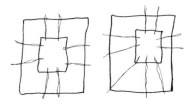

Fragment inserted in a frame.

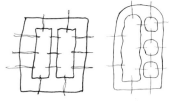

Experiment with shapes and positions in frames.

Right: Thick paper patches applied to Kunin (acrylic felt) using a built-in stitch. After zapping the felt some distortion can be seen.
Far right: Various papers applied to Kunin felt with free-form machine stitching and a built-in stitch. More distortion can be seen after zapping this sample.

Machine-stitched links

A heat-activated stabilizer or vanishing muslin, such as Thermogauze, is useful if you are linking or inserting fragments with free-form machine stitching. When Thermogauze is subjected to heat from a heat tool or an iron, it disintegrates. If the paper is flimsy, fit the Thermogauze in a frame, turn the frame upside down, and attach paper patches with temporary adhesive or pins. Free-form machine stitch between the edges of the paper. Remove from the frame and place on a heat-resistant surface. Then zap both sides with a heat tool until the Thermogauze turns brown and can be brushed away.

Another fabric to consider is Kunin, which is acrylic felt. When zapped with a heat tool, the surface distorts and partly disintegrates. Interesting effects are possible as remnants of the felt remain around the stitching and the paper will probably distort. Pin some paper patches to the felt and free-form machine stitch between the edges. Then place felt side uppermost on a heat-resistant surface and use a heat tool cautiously. The felt will start to distort and holes will appear. Turn it over to check your progress, and continue until you're happy with the result. You may find that you prefer the wrong side. It is advisable to work a test piece, as some colors react differently.

When using either of these fabrics experiment with the manner of stitching. For example:

- Stitch from edge to edge in a gently curving manner or with an angular zigzag. Then stitch across the linking stitches.
- Stitch from side to side continuously or in blocks of stitch, varying the density of stitch.

To insert a patch or fragment, cut or tear a paper frame large enough to encompass the fragment and allow for a gap. Fix both pieces to Kunin or Thermogauze and join with free-form machine stitching. Take the stitches right into the frame and, if the fragment has a motif or design, try to echo the shape with the stitching. Remove the Kunin or Thermogauze as described above.

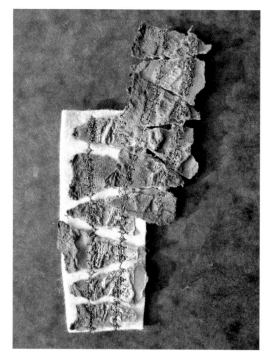

Crumpled and decorated brown (Kraft) paper, torn to form a frame, and small paper casts made using a molding mat were pinned to a piece of Thermogauze. They were linked with free-form machine stitching and the Thermogauze removed with a heat tool.

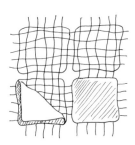

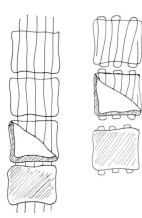

Structural links

By embedding threads between two sheets of wet-formed paper, you can link the paper as you make it or lay down the foundations for linking at a later stage. For example, make four sheets of paper and transfer two of them to a smooth or textured surface, leaving a gap in between. Cover both sheets of paper and the gap with several lengths of thread or string. Place the remaining two sheets of paper on top, cover with a felt and press with a roller. Paper can be linked vertically, horizontally, or diagonally into any arrangement using this technique.

The threads could form the foundation for composite stitches such as raised chain band, or for needle weaving.

A variation is to trickle a thread backward and forward across the paper, extending over the edges on opposite sides so that loops are formed. Cover with another sheet of paper and press as before. Several sheets of looped paper can then be laced together.

Yarn or wire sandwiched between two sheets of wet-formed paper to link several sheets together.

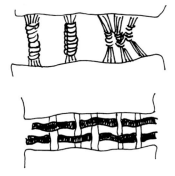

Laced links.

Wrapped and woven links.

A book created with paper cast on small slate tiles and linked with continuous threads. The linking threads were buttonholed and running stitch worked. The entire surface was sealed with gesso then colored with bright metallic paints. When dry, a coat of Liming wax (a Liberon product) was applied and then partially removed with clear wax.

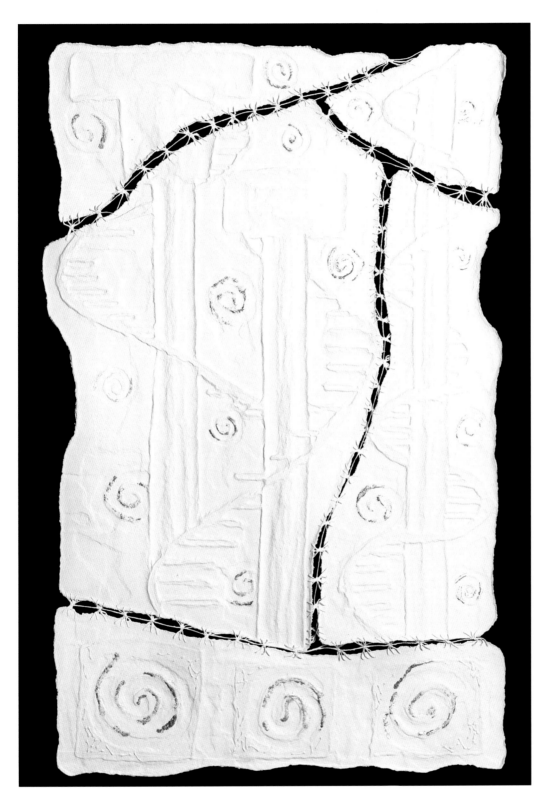

Reflections: 40 x 25 in (101 x 64 cm), inspired by Louise Bourgeois's installation Toi et Moi. A sheet of MDF was cut into sections and a mold built up with blotting paper. The cast was made using wet-formed paper and was removed from the mold while still damp so it would distort as it dried. The sections were laced together and the cast was painted with gesso with highlights in white gold leaf added.

Fusible thread and soluble film

Highly textured patches can be made using a combination of paper, fusible thread, and soluble film. The patches can be used separately or joined together.

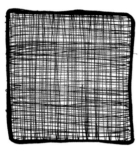

Frame wrapped with fusible thread.

Wrap a small frame quite densely from top to bottom then from side to side with Grilon or YLI fusible thread. Arrange a selection of torn papers on the frame. Cover with a piece of lightweight water-soluble film and tack or pin it in position. Set your machine for free-form stitching, with fusible thread on the bobbin and a metallic thread on top. Stitch around the inside of the frame to begin with then stitch within the frame, following the outline of the papers or doodling. Alternatively, you could draw a simple shape, pattern or design on the soluble film and stitch the outlines. Vary the density of stitch, leaving some areas unstitched to increase the distortion. Cut the threads and remove the patch from the frame. Fill a small container with hot water (just bearable) and immerse the patch. Allow it to shrivel up, then remove it from the water. Squeeze out the excess water and leave to dry. The water temperature is fairly critical. If it is too hot, the fusible thread disintegrates; if it is not hot enough there is little distortion. Experiment with different papers and paper thread, woven or layered paper, and different stitch patterns.

Torn paper placed over the fusible thread.

Paper covered with cold water soluble film and free-form machine stitched.

Fusible thread samples including:
Top left: A hexagonal frame was wrapped with fusible thread and a hexagonal spiral stitched heavily on the soluble film and paper.
Top middle: A design was drawn onto soluble film, torn papers were arranged fairly carefully, and the main lines stitched. Although distorted the design can be seen.

Cold water soluble film

Using lightweight cold water soluble film as a support for hand or machine stitch enables you to combine it with wet-formed paper or pulp, which will dissolve the film and leave the stitch element embedded in the paper. This technique can vary, so adopt an experimental approach—it will be well worthwhile. A variety of stitch effects can be created and additional material (fabric snippets, beads) can be added. A sticky residue is formed when the film dissolves, so check that the paper doesn't stick to the mold or felt.

Start with a simple experiment. Set your machine for free-form stitching and frame-up the soluble fabric. Cut several lengths of heavy metallic thread, form a grid on the soluble film, and couch using a free-form zigzag stitch. Change to a straight stitch and work a few diagonals or fill in some of the squares. Remove the film from the frame, trim any excess, and experiment with the following ideas.

- Sandwich the film between two thin sheets of wet-formed paper and press. Tear some of the paper away to reveal the stitch.
- Apply a release agent, line a mold with Mulberry or Lokta tissue and cover the film with wet-formed paper or pulp. The tissue can be distressed and partly removed with a wet brush (see page 26).
- Place the film on a piece of mesh and drop the pulp on top, partly covering the stitch.
- Combine hand and machine stitch on the soluble film and/or apply snippets of fabric, beads, or sequins.

Rectangles of copper shim were machine stitched together using cold water soluble film as a support. The film was placed on a piece of mesh and partly covered with pulp. When dry, copper wire and pierced, waxed brown paper were applied to the surface.

Weaving

Various weaving techniques can be employed to create or enhance paper surfaces and structures. Look at cloth and braid weaving or basketry for ideas to try out or adapt. Approach it experimentally. The woven element doesn't have to be regular or form the entire structure and other materials can be combined with paper.

- Wrap a small loom or frame with yarn, paper, thread, or wire and weave with strips of paper. Experiment with different types of paper. Use cut, torn, thick, thin, twisted, plaited, or woven strips and weave evenly, unevenly, create loops, or leave gaps and try any other variations you can think of. Remove the weaving from the loom or frame. Stabilize with iron-on interfacing, if you wish, and enrich with hand or machine stitch or apply to another surface.
- Cut slots in a sheet of paper or paper object and weave with cut or torn strips of paper, metal shim, or wire.
- Make a small weaving using wire for the warp, manipulate it into a pleasing shape and dip it in a vat containing pulp with fabric and thread snippets.

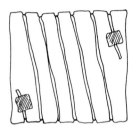

Card loom back.

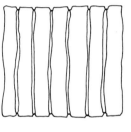

Card loom front.

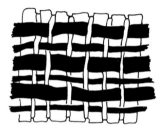

Card loom woven.

Paper cut, torn, and woven.

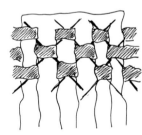

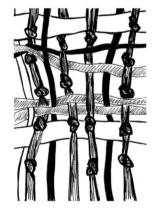

Various woven paper ideas.

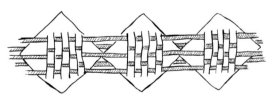

Paper squares with slots cut, woven together.

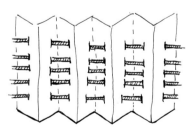

Paper cut, folded, and woven.

Examples of woven paper including:
Top: Paper and embossed copper shim woven and machine stitched to Kunin (acrylic felt) with fragments of *papier mâché* applied by hand.
Middle: Copper wire wrapped around a frame and woven with various papers. The wires were cut and twisted together.

Combining techniques

Cover a wire frame with yarn, twine, or string. Weave, wrap or work a design in needle-lace or macramé, leaving some areas open. Mix some pulp to a pouring consistency with water and PVA, then add metal leaf flakes, glitter, or sequins. Place the frame over a plastic container and pour the mixture over it carefully, building up some areas and allowing the underlying structure to show in others. While the pulp is wet, the surface can be impressed and ink, silk paints, or watercolor paint dropped onto the surface. Allow to dry before removing from the frame.

Pulp containing glitter and metal leaf flakes was poured over string wrapped unevenly around a metal frame. Brown ink was dripped onto the surface before the pulp dried.

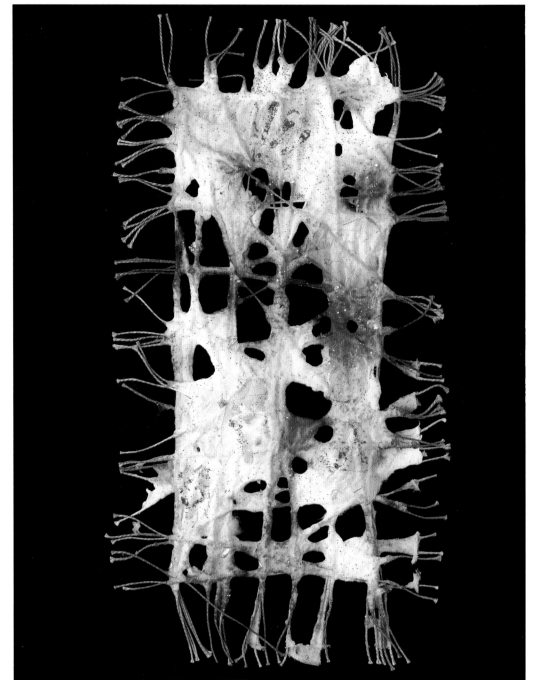

Have a selection of textured paper, bits of lace, and pearl thread in different weights (don't worry about color). Draw a pattern or design on a piece of brown (Kraft) paper, crumple it, then reinforce it with iron-on interfacing. Take long straight stitches, by hand, to pick out the main design lines in the heaviest-weight pearl. Don't try to follow the lines exactly but use them as a guide and interpret the design loosely. Add detail with lighter-weight threads and apply pieces of torn lace or textured paper to create areas of interest. Remember to leave some quiet areas to balance the design. Cover the surface with gesso and follow with a coat of acrylic paint. Then apply gilding wax or metal leaf and patinate, glaze, or distress, or try any of the decorative techniques from the previous chapter.

Use a textured mold or master to make a *papier mâché* vessel or small panel and either tear away one or more sections (to rejoin later) or leave the object whole. Place a sheet of Mulberry tissue on the mold or master and take several small rubbings. Tear the tissue to separate the rubbings, then reinforce with another piece of tissue. Select threads with a pronounced twist or slight texture and stitch, using the rubbings as a guide. The thread on both sides of the stitches will show when the tissue is adhered to another surface, so choose from running, whipped running, or Holbein (double running) stitches and avoid trailing threads or knots unless you want them to show.

Left: A design worked on crumpled brown paper in running and fly stitches with torn lace applied.
Right: The surface was sealed with gesso and painted with burnt umber acrylic. Copper wax was applied and left to dry. Black patinating wax and blue moods wax (Liberon products) were used to enrich the effect. Finally, copper was used to add highlights.

Papier mâché vessel.

Three sections torn away.

Mulberry tissue stitched and
adhered to a section.

Sections laced back into place.

Fix the tissue to the *papier mâché* object with PVA diluted half-and-half with water. Place the stitched pieces carefully and you will have an impression on one side and a stitched interpretation on the other. If you have torn sections from the object, rejoin by lacing or use an insertion stitch. Cover both sides of the object and any stitch with paint, gesso, texture gel or a combination, then decorate the surface using one of the techniques described in Chapter 3.

Moving on

We hope this experimental approach to paper and stitch will encourage you to explore the medium. This is really only the beginning, though. As you work with the techniques, you will gain confidence and start to make your own creative connections. Remember to adopt the "What if. . . ?" approach and remain open to new ideas. Look at products and techniques used in other crafts, for example, to see if you could adapt them for your own purposes.

Remember that many of the color and stitch techniques described in these first four chapters can be used with the metal explored in the next four chapters. Paper will also make an excellent background for the metal.

Papier mâché vessel, sections torn and rejoined with lacing and the design worked in Holbein (double-running) stitch. The vessel was decorated with the faux verdigris technique using a combination of copper wax and purple and turquoise acrylic paint (see page 45).

Part Two: Metal

5
Getting Started with Metal

Materials

A wide variety of metallic media can be used in stitched pieces. Probably the most common of these is the fine sheet metal called shim. This is fine enough to stitch and the thickness 0.05 mm is ideal for stitching. It is readily available in copper or brass. The copper tends to be softer and easier to use initially, so it is probably a good one to start with.

Recycling can be a good thing and you will find that the supermarket is a good place to start. Tomato, garlic, and onion purée often come in soft metallic tubes that can be reused when empty. Toothpaste tubes are mostly plastic now but the occasional brand still uses soft metal, so it's worth looking. These metals will not color in the same way as the commercial shim, but they are great for getting started. Obviously they will need to be cut open and cleaned well to get rid of any residue. Different brands have different colors and may be aluminum or could resemble brass or copper.

Aluminum sheets are sold in a variety of colors and these are very soft and easy to stitch. Again, they will not react to heat in the same way but can give good results.

Vegetable purée tubes, as shown here, can be used together with shim, flexible foils, copper blanks, a paper crinkler and wires. All these can be combined to make exciting embroideries.

Madonna Icon: 10 x 18 in (26 x 46 cm). Lazertran was used to put an image from a sketch book onto metal shim. Borders were formed from strips of shim and stitched with an automatic pattern. Wires, metals, and other media were used to complete the piece.

Wiremesh is, as the name suggests, quite a soft metal mesh. It comes in copper and brass, will color with heat and can be painted using any of the methods described in Chapter 6. It gives a much more subtle effect when stitched and this is often useful. It also works well when used in conjunction with the shinier metal shim.

Also available for use in textiles are the copper blanks that are usually sold for enameling in kilns. Wires can be used, either with the metal or on their own, and they are great for adding accents or wrapping the heavier metal pieces.

Other materials that we explore here are patination agents to age the metal, embossing powders to texture it, a variety of paints for different purposes, and Lazertran, a plastic film that enables images to be permanently placed on the metal.

Free-form machine stitching can be used to build the metal into an embroidery. Any machine will do as long as it has straight stitch and zigzag options. It is quite safe to stitch into the shim. Handstitching is also possible.

The backing for this piece was distressed velvet with Wiremesh. Hand and machine stitching were built up to integrate the background. Metal shim was stitched on felt, cut out, and placed over the top as a focal point. Finally, Wireform was stitched behind the piece and the sides curled.

Copper and brass in real metal, whether shim or Wiremesh, change color quite dramatically when heat is applied. The best way to do this is to hold it in a flame or over an electric plate. Do be sure that this is done safely. A candle works well, although it does make the metal sooty (but this residue will wipe away afterwards). Always use candles near a sink or a large bowl of water. A gas-cooker flame is quicker and a camping gas stove can be used, provided it is on a very stable surface and care is taken. A mini blowtorch can be purchased for use in the kitchen, and this is ideal.

To color the metal, wear an oven glove to hold it in tongs. Remember that the metal will retain the heat for quite a long time, so be careful to lay it on a heat-resistant surface when

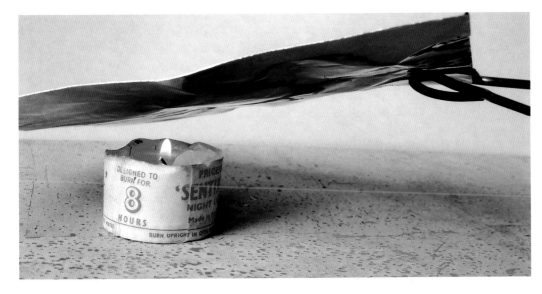

coloring is done and allow it to cool completely before touching it. Introduce the metal to the flame gradually and watch it carefully. Pull back as it starts to change color and do not overheat or you will lose the color. Copper in particular gives some wonderful colors, from deep pink to a bluey-green. Allow some of the original color to remain. Wait until it is cool to the touch.

The next step is to emboss a design in the metal.

Embossing the metal shim

Metal shim and purée tubes are malleable. Lines and texturing marks can be drawn into the surface. This is called embossing and it creates a texture. Metal is very shiny and this can cause problems when integrating it into an embroidery. Textured areas help to reduce the shine. Wiremesh does not hold an impression and is not suitable for embossing.

For the basic method, you will need metal shim or a fine metal purée tube and an embossing tool, although an old ballpoint pen that has run out of ink, or a knitting needle, could be used instead. It is best to think ahead about the design for the pattern that is to be placed on the metal. A tracing will work well or a copy of a design from your sketchbook. You can, of course, make freehand lines and shapes but it is often easier to plan in advance.

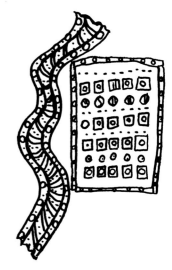

Suitable designs for tracing onto metal shim.

Decide which side you like best and lay the metal *right-side down* on a soft surface such as a mouse mat. These are available at computer stores. If you can't get one then use a magazine or newspaper. Lay the paper with the design on the metal and draw over the lines with the embossing tool or pen. You can press quite hard at this stage. Remove the paper when the main lines have been drawn and draw over the lines again. This time press hard but not so hard that you puncture the metal. The right side will be the reverse of the metal—the side with the raised line. Bear this in mind when using lettering.

Add texture by drawing little dashes or by stabbing with the tool to make dots. This gives a stippled effect. Practice on a spare piece of metal to get the feel of this technique as it is easy to puncture the metal. Think about and try other marks that add texture. You will see how machining into the shim adds marks and textures, too. You may not like the extreme shine of the metal, so it helps to paint the embossed surface with black acrylic paint, then wipe it off immediately with paper towels. The paint settles into the embossing lines and dulls the shine. More on this later.

Shapes could be cut from the metal and these could also be embossed. Metal leaves, for instance, could have their vein lines drawn in and some areas could be stippled to add texture. Consider also using the metals for borders. These could be made up from individually shaped pieces that echo the overall theme of the work.

Below: Embossed leaf shapes and stippled metal.

Stitching by machine

Chapter 7 contains lots of ideas for stitching, but for those who can't wait to get started, here are some initial suggestions. Metal shim and purée tubes can be stitched using an ordinary sewing machine. The stitching raises some areas of the metal, producing a quilted look. The thread color tints the metal and some of the variegated threads can produce lovely color effects. Free-form machine stitching techniques work well and, if your machine has some built-in stitches, these can also be used.

There is no need to use a particularly large needle as this would make too big a hole as it stitched. On the other hand, a large needle mark may be just what your project needs, so try a variety and see which works for you. The metal does not seem to cause needles to break but, if you don't already wear glasses, it is advisable to use safety glasses to protect the eyes. All machines are individual, so be prepared to try different needle sizes. Keep a needle specifically for working on metal as inevitably it will blunt slightly. The single most important thing is to base the work on as thick an interfacing as you can find: craft-weight Vilene (or other interfacing) is good. The reason for this is that the metal may snag the thread as the needle goes through it. The craft Vilene will absorb this and prevent the thread from breaking.

Start your experiments with stitch using plain metal, not embossed, to get used to the feel of it.

1   Place some fabric—painted silk or velvet—on a piece of craft Vilene or other heavy interfacing. Use temporary adhesive spray to hold it in place.

2   Cut some heat-colored metal into shapes—squares, triangles, or similar—and arrange on the fabric in a pattern that pleases you. Use temporary adhesive spray to hold the metal while you stitch.

3   Set up the machine for free-form stitching and thread with a suitable color or a variegated thread. If the thread breaks, try a slightly stronger one. Use any thread in the bobbin. A frame should not be needed as the craft Vilene is quite thick.

4   Begin to stitch using free running stitch and working in a flowing motion across the shape. Leave little gaps between the stitching and note the effect. Refer to the diagram below for stitch direction.

5   Stitch around the edge of the shape, using a thread in a similar color to the fabric to integrate the shapes. Nibble into the edges with machine stitch to make borders.

Some of the ways in which the metal could be stitched.

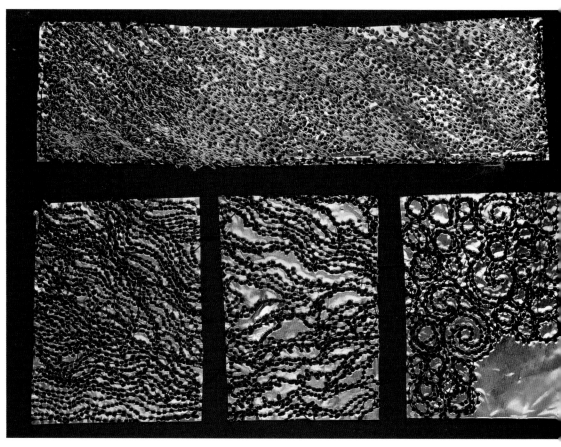

You can see from this picture how the direction of the stitch affects the result. The long strip shows how the thread color influences the metal. Several variegated colors were used here.

This is the basic method of stitching into the shim. If you stitch into the embossed metal, make sure that you stitch within the shape and not across the embossed lines. For instance, the photo of the leaves on the previous page shows how the stitching runs along between the embossed veins and doesn't cross them.

The best way of learning about the metal is to experiment with the stitching. Make samples using lots of different threads and vary the stitching—small circles of free running stitch work well to integrate the metal. Use some plain and some embossed metal pieces. This will provide a useful reference piece.

Stitching by hand

It is quite possible to stitch the metal by hand although this is more limited in application. However, if you are a handstitcher, here are a few ideas for applying the metal.

1   Start with a small square of heat-colored metal and emboss a design. Cut a piece of sheer fabric larger than the metal. Very fine chiffon, such as a scarf, will hardly show at all but denser fabrics will add color. Then place the metal on the background, lay the sheer fabric on top and stitch around the edges to trap the metal in a pocket. The stitching could be in a thread that matches the background so that it almost disappears, or in a contrasting color to add emphasis to the shape. Other shapes could of course be used and the edges of the covering fabric could be frayed.

2   Stitch through the metal shape around the edges to attach it. It may be necessary to make holes in the shim with a large, sharp needle (press through the metal onto a mouse mat or similar surface) and stab stitch up and down through these holes

to fix the metal. This edge could be of decorative stitching or you could couch ribbon, beads, or crinkled metal around the edges of the shim to cover them and make a decorative feature

3 Work random handstitches, using quite a thick yarn, all over the metal. The metal should gleam through the stitching and be allowed to show in some places. This can be achieved by stitching with a big needle or by piercing the metal first and using these holes. Prepunched holes can be placed to integrate with your design.

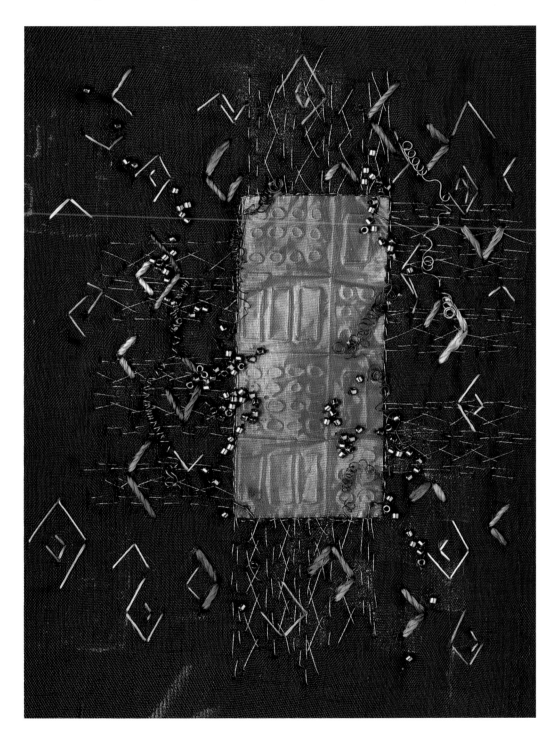

Byzantine: 6 x 8 in (15 x 20 cm). This piece of work by Maureen Beale is a good example of how to hand stitch the metal. A sheer fabric was laid over embossed metal shim with hand stitching and beads used to integrate the metal. The underlying velvet was block printed before stitching to add interest.

These little patches show ideas for hand stitching. They were placed on handmade embossed paper.

Some of the ways in which metal could be stitched.

Running stitch.   Buttonholed edges and beads.   Wrapped pipe cleaner.   Crinkled metal strips.

Paper crinkler

Using a paper crinkler on metal gives some really exciting effects. Buy the strongest one that you can. Start by cutting the metal into long strips and putting them through the crinkler. Then try some of the following.

- Couch down the resulting strip to the fabric by taking a stitch in the ditch—the depression formed by the crinkler.
- Use bugle beads stitched across the strip to nestle in the depressions made by the crinkler.
- Try pinching the pleats close together on one side to make a curve before couching and beading.
- Cut into a crinkled strip with scissors and note the interesting edge this produces.
- Plaiting several crinkled strips together is fun. Plait them so that they lie fairly flat. Couch to a backing fabric or use as an edging. Several of these strips couched down close to each other with beads can look very rich.

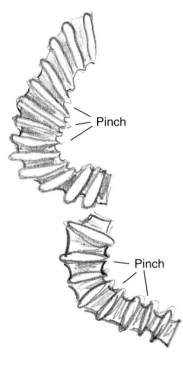

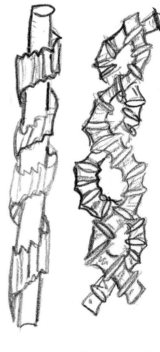

Pinch the crinkled strips into shapes.	Stitch with bugles in the depressions.	With round beads.	Wrapped around a painted straw.	Two crinkled strips wound together.

Cut triangles from shim or Wiremesh and put them through the crinkler. Then squeeze them together at the base, as shown on the following page, to make shapes with an Art Deco look. These could have small holes made in them so that they can be attached to fabric. They also make very good tassels when attached to wires.

Brooches could be made by stitching these to fabric and adding beads, before stretching over card stock shapes.

Sampler showing the use of a paper crinkler. Thin strips were curled and wider strips bent into curves with some beading. Some small pieces have been pinched into fan shapes. Cutting the strips with scissors made interesting edges.

More ideas for using the paper crinkler. Some pieces have been pinched into small fan-shaped tassels. These could be made into brooches.

Using wire

Coiled wire techniques

The inclusion of wire spirals complement and enhance your stitched metal. They can be useful in many ways and are easy to make. The addition of beads to the wire adds to their attraction. They are made from quite thin wire, mostly thin enough to be workable by hand. There are many thicknesses of wire to be found at specialist shops but craft shops and garden centers can be useful, too. Florists' wire is inexpensive, comes in many lovely colors, and is ideal for coiled wire techniques. Enameled wire is also good but tends to be more expensive. Thick garden wire is usually green but it takes a metallic spray very well. This is good for heavier pieces.

To make a shape from wire similar to those shown on the left, cut off a suitable length—about 10 in (25 cm) is a good average. Using a small pair of needlenose pliers, grab the wire as close to one end as possible and fold it over itself to make a loop. Adjust the loop so that it is as small as you can make it. Then, with the pliers across the loop and holding it firmly, begin to wind the wire around the loop. If you want a tight spiral, wind slowly, a fraction of a millimeter at a time. It will build up surprisingly quickly. When you reach halfway along the wire, start at the other end. However you start, you will probably finish with both spirals on the same side. Don't worry—just twist the wire until they are on opposite sides, as shown left.

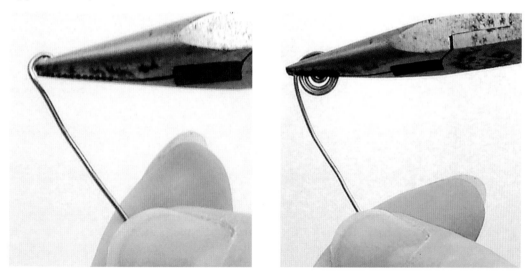

Far left: Shaping the wire loop is not difficult; here is the initial loop.
Left: The loop has now been wound and is almost completed.

This is just the beginning. There is no limit to the shapes you can make with wire—and a great many different types of wire. One variation is to place beads in the middle—just remember to do so before you start winding from the second end. This is very effective when added to embroidery, as the beads give emphasis to the thinner wires. The whole piece can then be stitched into place; it is best to do this by hand.

A different effect can be achieved by hammering the wire flat. Lay it on a solid surface—you can buy mini-anvils from silversmiths' shops or discount stores—and hammer steadily until it is quite flat. A simple twist, made with two different-colored wires, will resemble chain stitch when flattened in this way.

The wires add detail to the borders. A simple strip of metal, stitched with an open pattern, can become quite exotic when a series of beaded hearts is added.

Opposite page: This shows various wire shapes. Some of them have beads and some have been twisted together before winding. Others have been hammered to flatten them.

Right: Border taken from the *Madonna Icon* on page 69. The detail shows a stitched strip of metal with a built-in pattern used to provide some detail. Coiled wire was made into heart shapes with beads at the point of the heart. Roundels of stitched shim show the effect of the patination fluids.

Opposite above: Copper blanks (left) were decorated using spirit dyes and embossing powders (right). Some of the embossed ones had stamps pressed into them while the embossing powder was hot.

Opposite below: This detail of a vessel by Rachel Catlow shows glass pieces, as used by florists, trapped inside wire cages. Rachel's clever idea could be used in a variety of ways.

Working with thicker metal

Thicker metals cannot be stitched in the same way as the shim. They can, however, be cut out to make domes or strips. These heavier shapes are great to provide a change of scale and weight. Strips of heavier metal can be cut with tin snips and coiled like the wire.

Copper blanks

What are copper blanks? They are shaped pieces of thicker copper, about 0.66 mm. Craft workers who enamel copper in kilns often use these copper shapes as a basis for their enameling process. They can be quite useful for us as well, although they are usually much too thick to manipulate or shape. They come in interesting shapes and sizes and it is well worth keeping your eyes open for them. You can often find them in craft shops.

First of all, decorate the copper blanks. This can be by any of the methods described in Chapter 6. They work particularly well with embossing powders and stamped images.

When decorated and completely dry, wrap with a heavy wire to secure the shape. If you are attaching one of the domes or beaten shapes discussed below, you may find that you need to wrap the wire in two directions and secure the middle with a stitch. See diagram to the left for an explanation.

In fact, it can be very interesting to work buttonhole stitch over the wires to add a stitched element to the metal. Whichever way you decide to do it, make sure your shape is very firmly enclosed in the wire cage and won't come out. Then just stitch in place through the wire, stab stitching to your background going up and down around the edge of the shape, into the wire and down the other side. An alternative to the wire would be to drill the shapes.

Wire wrapped around copper blank.

The blanks shown in the photograph on page 83 were wrapped with wire and stitched to a background of distressed velvet. Some shell fragments were applied in the same way.

Sampler

Consolidate all that you have learned in this chapter by making a small sampler. Choose an interesting background fabric, maybe velvet, paper, or painted silk. Place the background fabric on a heavy craft Vilene (interfacing) background, using Wonder Under (fusible webbing) or a temporary adhesive spray to hold it in place. Cut shapes from the heat-colored, embossed metal and arrange them on the fabric. When you are happy with the arrangement, spray the back of the first piece of metal with the temporary adhesive. This will hold it for long enough for you to apply the shape. Spray the shapes one at a time as you stitch them. Add strips of crinkled metal or coiled wire. Think about the edges: turn them under, burn them, or use plaited, crinkled strips as a border.

Sampler with Fish: 7 x 10 in (18 x 26 cm). This embroidery used many of the techniques shown so far in the book. The background was handmade paper. A shaped piece of metal was crinkled using the paper crinkler, and leaves and fish shapes were used in the design, which flows with the paper.

6

Coloring the Metal

Stitching into metal shim opens new avenues for embroiderers but you soon realize that the very shiny surface of the metal brings its own problems. Embossing the metal, or adding texture by using a tool or by stitching, can help to 'knock back' the shine but it can still be too dominant and overpower the piece of work. The answer is to color the metal using a variety of media. Starting with a simple antiquing technique using acrylic paint, this chapter offers lots of ideas for coloring the metal prior to stitching. All these methods will work on Wiremesh, too.

Many agents can be used to color the metal. These range from a simple store-cupboard solution like vinegar to a highly specific treatment such as a chemical compound that ages and patinates the metal. Various dyes can be used on the metal and you can even use your own designs from your sketchbook to transfer as an image. Most of the easily available materials are covered here, but there are many more compounds that can be used.

Masks and stencils

Bear in mind, when trying the coloring options, that the metal can be masked before applying the color media. This could be done by drawing on the metal with PVA glue or painters' masking fluid. Allow to dry before painting. The mask can be removed by peeling away or scraping off after the color has dried. The PVA also looks good left on, and can be sponged through a stencil, or a stamp could be dipped into it (brush it out onto glass to make a dipping surface). You'll find more suggestions in the relevant sections, but the PVA method works for most coloring media. As you can see from the photo (right), it can also be painted and gilded to form part of the design or used as an edge.

Vinegar solutions

Good results can be obtained with ordinary household vinegar. Just sprinkle some malt vinegar on the shim. To get good color variation, work with metal that has previously been heated. Put the metal into a plastic freezer bag and ruche the bag. Leave for two days, then remove from the bag and rinse to remove the vinegar. You should have some interesting effects where the vinegar acid has etched the metal. Another exciting option is to try dark balsamic vinegar, using the freezer bag as before; it should result in some interesting and unusual colors, as you can see from the photo opposite. Here are some variations on this technique.

- Press a rubber or foam stamp on the metal when it is placed in the bag. A small stencil will work, too.
- Mix Procion dye (or other fiber-reactive dye) with the vinegar. Wear mask and gloves when mixing the dye.
- Emboss with some deep lines before soaking.

This shows how the metal can be masked with PVA glue (top left). Spirit soluble dyes were then painted over the PVA and, in the top right photograph, the PVA was then removed. The bottom right piece was painted with the PVA remaining in place. The PVA glue was also used to edge the small sample, which was then painted with acrylics.

A sketchbook was used to record the results of coloring experiments. This page shows what happened when the shim was coated with balsamic vinegar.

Acrylic paints and patinating waxes

Acrylic paint can be used to color areas of metal shim. One of the most effective ways of doing this is to start with an embossed motif and, with a medium-width paintbrush, paint all over it with black paint, working the paint into the cracks and crevices. Then, using paper towels, immediately wipe it off. Sufficient paint will stay in the deeply embossed areas to give an aged effect. This is even more effective if the metal has been colored with heat first.

Roxelana: 15 x 8 in (38 x 20 cm). This embroidery of the Ottoman empress used computer transfer techniques with water-soluble fabric. The frame was made from embossed shim, which was lightly coated with black acrylic paint.

Detail of *Roxelana,* showing how the acrylic paint was applied and then wiped off, giving an antique finish.

Setacolor Tagger paint was sprayed onto embossed metal. Acrylic paint was then used to darken it.

This look can be varied by using other colors in the acrylic paint. For an antique look, dark colors are best. You could also try dry-brushing a bright color over the raised area when the first coat of dark acrylic has dried. Keep the paint layer quite light—if you apply too much it will flake off. Setacolor spray paints also work well on metal. Use two or three colors and allow to mix.

A similar effect can be obtained using special patinating waxes. The black one is most useful and gives an effect similar to the dark paint. Paint it on, then rub it off after a few minutes. Waxes can be useful with the embossed metal to define the design. They can be used in conjunction with most of the coloring methods that follow. Allow the acrylic paint to dry before trying other coloring agents.

Chemical patination agents

Chemical patination agents can be used to distress the metal, but care should be taken with these as they can be dangerous if inhaled. It's probably best to wear a mask and certainly to wear rubber gloves. What happens with these is that the fluid is painted on the metal and then, over a period of time, the patination agent (which is clear when applied) turns them into a verdigris-type green. I like them best used on metal that has been colored by the heat, embossed, and defined with dark acrylic. There are certain things to remember.

- The patination can be very obvious. It's better to work up several coats rather than apply heavily in one session.
- The chemical reacts with the metal and a colored residue forms (verdigris, rust, or black). The rust has a tendency to rub off. The black works very quickly and can be too heavy. Try diluting it with water. It's great used with the blue or green effects when those are used first.

The finish is not permanent for any of the fluids although the blue, green, and black do last very well. Using matt acrylic varnish will set the color but may change the look of the surface.

It is worth remembering that the patination fluids work on any metal surface and it is quite possible to buy paint that contains metal. Make sure that the paints you buy are especially for combining with the patination fluids.

Patination fluids were used for the strip at the top of this picture. The other strips were colored with faux verdigris, which mixes paint with denatured alcohol.

You can use patination fluids on almost any surface. You could block-print, using metal paint on fabric and dabbing with the patination fluid afterwards. It works particularly well when combined with water-soluble paper on metal and can give some interesting effects. There is more about stitching into water-soluble paper in Chapter 7.

You will find that the mix of acrylic paint and denatured alcohol technique given on page 45 will work well on metal, too. We call this faux verdigris.

Spirit-soluble dyes

Care should be taken with these dyes. They are flammable, so beware naked flames and do not use without wearing a mask and gloves.

These dyes are often called wood dyes and they react with denatured alcohol (DA) to produce some interesting effects. They are not easily obtained and, although you can sometimes find them in craft or do-it-yourself stores, they are likely to be in limited, woody shades. In the Resources section on pages 126 and 127, we give mail-order sources where you can get the bright colors. Just paint them on and see the results. Mix the colors. Now add a little DA to the brush and smudge it onto the painted surface. It's very exciting to see the effects. It is also interesting to paint with one color and then mix another color with DA and paint back into the first. Prop the metal up and allow the color to run.

These two strips of embossed metal show the results of using spirit-soluble dye. They were distressed with DA.

Glass paints

It is quite possible to use glass paints or nail polish on metal shim. They come in wonderful bright colors and the shine of the metal through the paint can give quite an exciting, extraordinary finish. There are many varieties of glass paint but the one I like best is a bit like painting with warm jelly.

It is best to paint all over a surface, perhaps heating the metal to color it first. Apply the glass paints using a sponge, allowing the colors to run into each other. Give them a good long time to dry. Paint the metal first and then draw any embossing designs into it afterwards. The effects of the paints merging together with the lines running through to join them can be quite extraordinary and well worth pursuing. Stitching must be done a long, long time after the paint has dried, so allow some time for this technique. Give it a good week to dry before stitching into the surface.

You can also use these paints on the embossed, acrylic wiped, designs. Paint in the specific areas and allow to dry. Then rub with a little wax to soften the effect.

This detail, which forms a decorative panel on a book, shows the exciting results that can be achieved using glass paints and nail polish. The rectangles of shim were stitched to paper with a central area of woven strips. The metal was painted after stitching.

Another glass painting material is called Pebeo (Crystal) Gel. These are lovely, translucent gels, which come in many colors and are particularly good with metal. Build up in thin layers by painting the gel all over one piece of metal, then put another piece of metal on top and pull it away. You will be left with a very organic pattern. When dry, repeat with another color. These gels aren't as obvious as the glass paints or as brightly colored, but they can have a very subtle gleam of their own, especially when the metal underneath is colored and this shows through.

Using embossing powders with metal

Embossing powders are generally used by rubber stampers to raise their designs above the surface. They can be very effective on metal provided that a sticking agent ensures that the embossing powder sticks to the metal. The sticking agent could be a wax, a paint that can be heated, or Pebeo (Crystal) Gel.

Wax

Just rub the wax quite heavily over the metal, and sprinkle lightly with embossing powder. Shake off any remnants onto a piece of paper (they can go back into the embossing powder pot). Then use a heat tool to raise the areas of embossing powder. You will find that you can create different effects depending upon how thickly you sprinkle the powder.

Paints and gels

Embossing powders can also be used over paint as long as it is safe to heat. It is worth finding out (don't try it with anything you are not sure about)—the Stewart Gill range are advertised as being suitable. Pebeo Gels, as discussed on the previous page, are particularly safe as they are designed to go into the oven. Just dab or brush on the Pebeo Gel, sprinkle over the embossing powder, shake it off and heat it, as before.

Stamps

It is quite possible to use rubber stamps or wooden blocks to put motif designs on metal. For this, brush the Pebeo Gel onto a thick piece of glass or plastic glass so that you have a surface pool to dip the stamp into. Then place your stamp, face down, in the Pebeo Gel and transfer it by placing it carefully (just tap it down) on the metal. Lift it off cleanly, cover with the embossing powder, shake off the excess, and heat as you did before. You will find

This piece of brass shim was first stitched, then wax was applied and embossing powders were shaken over the stitching and heated. After this, the piece was given a further coating of wax and Pearl Ex powders.

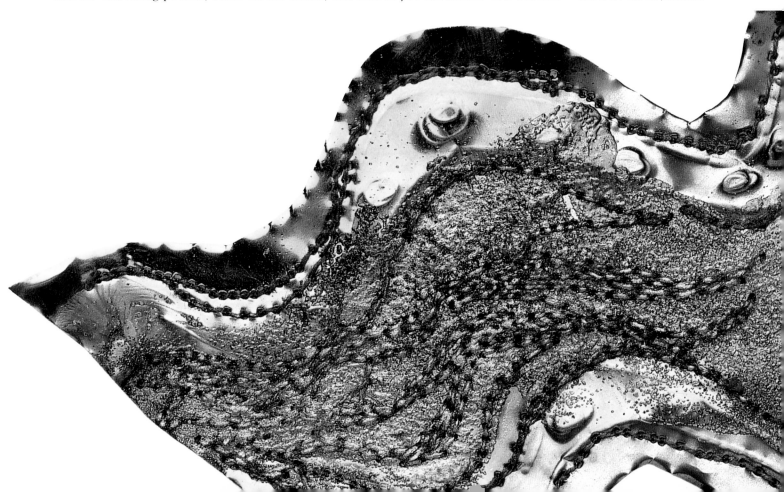

that the stamp has created an interesting surface on top of the metal. Alternatively, heat several layers of embossing powder by shaking more powder on after heating and then push an inked stamp into it. This will give a deep impression.

Try adding effects like wax with colored Pearl Ex powders or black patinating wax over the top of the stamped image, to add definition.

A molding mat was used on this metal, stamped with black Staz-on (designed for difficult surfaces) ink. The top piece shows what happens if you then use embossing powder and press the stamp into it. The middle and lower ones show the effect of just the stamp with the ink and some slight crinkling and stitching. Wrapped pipe cleaners add interest.

Decorating the metal with Lazertran

Lazertran is a paper product. You take your image and a sheet of Lazertran to the photocopy shop where they copy your image onto the paper using their laser color copier (it doesn't work with a black-and-white copier, even if the image is black and white—and it may damage the copier). It is almost impossible to do this at home, even with a laser printer. It just won't work. There are particular photocopiers that it works with (it tells you this on the packet). Although this makes it an expensive medium, it is really the best way of transferring your image onto metal.

This diagram shows suitable designs for placing on shim using the Lazertran transfer method. Sometimes the outlines are lost when the design is placed onto the metal and you will note that on the figures, the outline has been exaggerated using an ordinary ballpoint pen.

You can see here the Lazertran process. Top left is the original design on paper. Top right is the design transferred to Lazertran and floated off onto the metal. The two little photos bottom left show what happens when this is heated, and the piece on the right shows a small embroidery made using the Lazertran.

Float the Lazertran off in water (just like a children's transfer), place it on the metal and dab gently with a paper towel until all the water has come out of it. Leave it overnight to allow it to dry thoroughly. When that's done, heat it, either with an iron or a heat tool, or put it in the oven, and the plastic coating disappears, leaving the toner to color the metal. So it's not a surface technique but it actually lays color right into the metal.

It is possible to use any design, such as a photograph, computer image, or a drawing from your sketchbook. If you use an image from a book, make sure that it is copyright free. Don't take anybody else's work—it's just not worth it.

It is well worth coloring the metal with heat first. This adds a lot of interest as you see the metal coming through the colors of the Lazertran.

There are certain things to bear in mind when using Lazertran. For instance, any areas that are without color in the original image will become completely transparent and just show the color of the metal. Some colors, if they are metal-colored (oranges and, to some extent, yellows), might be absorbed and will not show up well. A dark, well-defined image comes through the best. Some of the images shown on page 95 will give you an idea of the results.

To use Lazertran successfully:

1   Cut out the design copied onto Lazertran and float it in a bowl of water. Take it out and, very carefully, check that the top plastic is sliding off the backing paper.

2   Lift it off, lay it onto your metal, dab very, very gently with a paper towel and then leave it completely alone overnight. If you don't allow the time, you will find there is water trapped underneath and, when you apply heat, it will make bubbles in the plastic that will pop. Sometimes, of course, this makes an exciting image and you might like the effect of the popped bubble, so it's well worth trying a piece to see what happens.

3   Now follow the pack instructions for heating. Either heat in an oven (preferably not one you cook food in) or place it on a heat-resistant surface and use a heat tool until the metal becomes shiny and scratching the image does not affect the color. Be careful when picking it up—allow it time to cool.

4   When you have heated it and the plastic has all disappeared, you can then consider taking it through to stitch as described in Chapter 7.

One thing that you might consider is combining a Lazertranned image (when the Lazertran has been heated and firmly set on the metal) with any of the above methods for coloring metal. For instance, using the shellac and paint method, you could just paint some areas of the image as though a verdigris effect has started but has not completely covered the image. This could give interesting effects. The glass paints also work particularly well, carefully painted over part of the image.

I have used Lazertran to put a series of icon images from my sketchbook on metal. As it can be used on any surface it is possible to place complementary designs on the frame used with the embroidery, linking the two together.

7

Into Metal with Stitch

We covered the very basic elements of stitching into metal in Chapter 5. If you always remember to have a weighty fabric as a base for the metal (and craft Vilene or other interfacing is ideal for this), you will be able to stitch without constant thread breaks. For happy stitching, make sure that the thickness of the metal is not greater than 0.05 mm. The copper is easier to work into than the brass for stitching as it is softer. Copper can always be heated to produce a gold color if that is needed. Metal can be used in embroidery in so many ways. Small pieces can be used to add accents or larger, embossed areas could form the main focus of the work. Lazertran can be used for detailed images, such as the icon shown below.

One of the main advantages of stitching into the metal is that the stitching automatically knocks back the shine. This is one of the results that we are aiming for. In this chapter, we look at stitching on different surfaces, adding wires and manipulated metal pieces, and making borders and patches to build up embroideries.

Dark Matter Angel 2: 9 x 13 in (23 x 33 cm). This icon image was transferred using Lazertran. The background fabric is craft Vilene bonded with tissue paper. A cut-out border runs along the left of the piece and small patches were applied to provide a finishing touch.

Opposite: *Coffee Grid*: 36 x 54 in (92 x 122 cm) by Anna Nowicki (detail). This embroidery has a waxed and varnished paper background. Further paper, in a distressed grid, was applied and the whole embellished with small boxes made from heated aluminum drinks cans. In some areas, a sewing machine was used without thread to make marks.

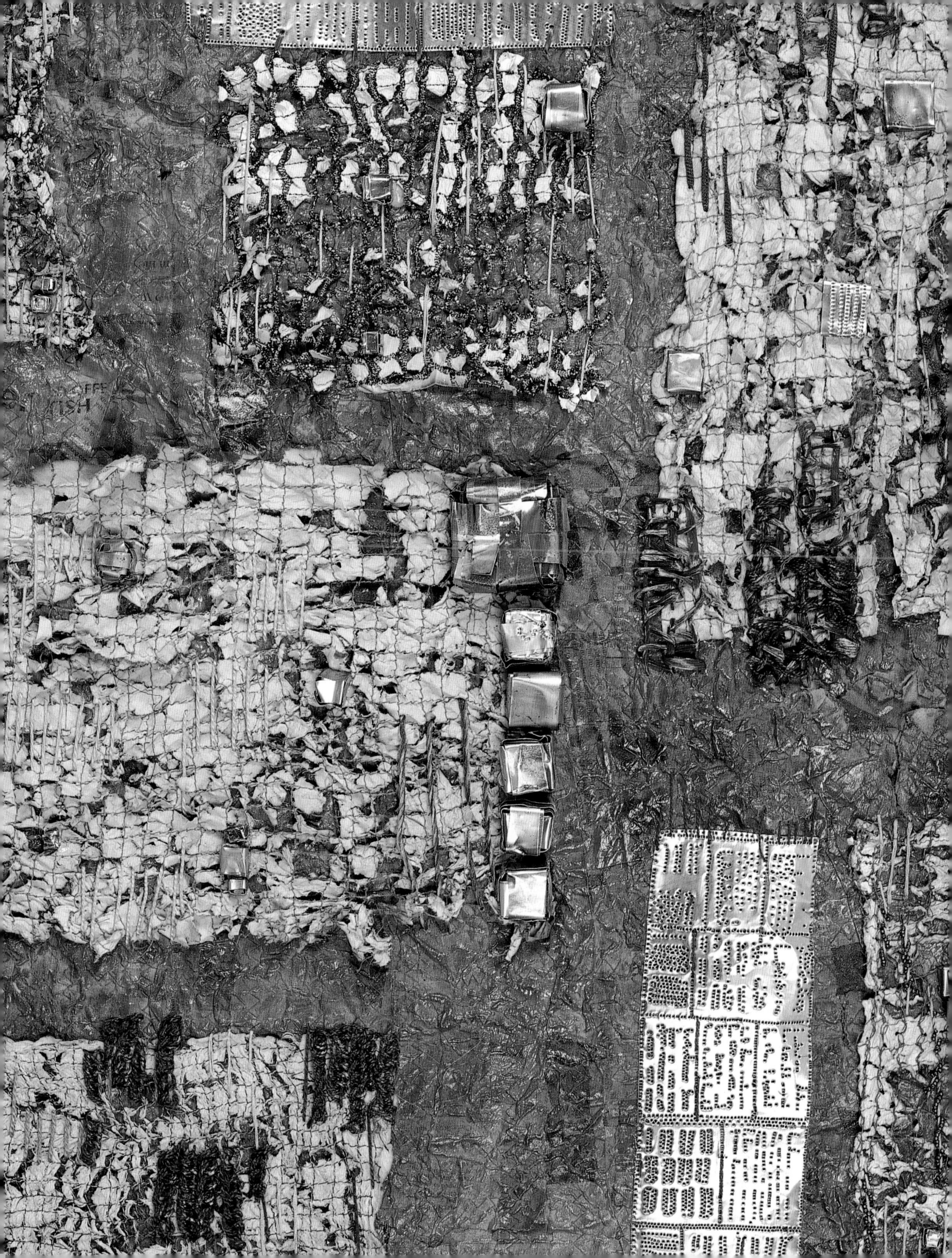

Iron the Transfoil (or other metallic transfer foil) onto fusible webbing on velvet with the side of the iron, not transferring too much of the foil.

Backgrounds for metal

Within reason, any fabric can be used as a background, provided the heavy craft Vilene is used underneath it. Particular personal favorites are velvet, handmade paper, and bonded tissue paper.

Velvet

The use of velvet with the metal can produce pieces of great subtlety, especially if the velvet is textured prior to stitching. A distressed look can give a suggestion of antiquity and can be achieved by ironing Wonder Under (fusible webbing) onto the velvet, adding some metallic glints with transfer foil and distressing with a heat tool.

Try the following:

1 Cut some acrylic velvet to the size needed. Cut a piece of Wonder Under (fusible webbing) slightly smaller than the velvet. Iron it onto the pile side of the fabric.

2 Lower the iron temperature to silk and place the transfer foil on top, shiny side up.

3 Use the side of the iron, as shown (left), to transfer the foil to the Wonder Under. Don't use too much foil or it will be too "glitzy."

4 Then use a heat tool to melt the Wonder Under and distress the foil.

5 Place on a firm background and work random free running stitch into the velvet.

Alternatives could involve using painted Wonder Under or stitching a layer of chiffon over the top of the velvet and zapping again with a heat tool.

Use this as a background to a small, precious stitched piece. The effect of shaped motifs stitched into the velvet is very special.

A selection of foiled velvet backgrounds, some of them made using stencils through which aerosol webbing was sprayed before the Transfoil was applied.

Paper

Handmade paper, as discussed in Chapters 1–4, is great as a support for the metal. It can be painted, using any medium, dyed with indigo or Procion dye or tea-dyed to give a delicate wash of color. It is particularly good if found objects are embedded into the paper at the making stage. There are some good ideas for this on page 25. A light spray of gold, before dyeing, gives super results.

These pieces of handmade paper were lightly sprayed with a metallic gold spray before dyeing with Procion dyes. This allowed the dye to penetrate from the back and gave an interesting effect on the top.

Tissue backgrounds. These background pieces were stamped after tissue paper was applied to the craft Vilene. Embossing powder was then added to the stamps to give a raised effect. Some were painted, some inked and bleached and some dyed with tea.

Tissue paper

Another technique with paper is to use Wonder Under (fusible webbing) to apply tissue paper to craft Vilene. This is very simple. Just cut a piece of Vilene, a piece of Wonder Under, and tissue paper slightly larger than the Vilene. Iron the webbing onto the Vilene and remove the backing paper. Then gently crumple the tissue and press it onto the warm Wonder Under, not smoothing out the creases. Iron well, using waxed paper to protect the iron. The result is a durable fabric that can be painted, tea-dyed, inked and bleached, stamped or stencilled. Try rubbing a little metallic wax, such as Treasure Gold, over it (very lightly) to pick out the creases.

Into stitch

Here are some ideas for stitching metal onto the backgrounds. These ideas work with any of the backgrounds described above.

Cut-out shapes

Drawn shapes for metal cutouts.

Shaped pieces of metal are very effective when integrated with the background. Work as follows:

1   Cut a piece of craft Vilene to go under the background fabric. If necessary, attach the fabric to the Vilene with a little random free-form machine stitching.

2   Now draw or trace a suitable motif on the metal. Choose an interesting shape, such as those shown on the left.

3 Place the drawing over the metal and transfer the lines. Remove the paper and draw again to reinforce the embossed lines. Cut out the shape, leaving a ¼ in (6 mm) border.

4 Make more motifs, as required. Perhaps some longer pieces could be made as borders.

5 Place on the background and arrange in a pleasing design.

6 Begin attaching by stitching in the middle of the metal. Hold down with temporary adhesive spray and stitch in place, taking care to integrate the motifs well into the background. Use a toning thread, slightly darker than the background. Stitch the central areas, too.

7 Complete the piece by stitching the shaped metal borders. You could also use the borders discussed on page 109.

Cut-out shapes can also be used with water-soluble paper or fabric. Follow the above instructions for embossing but place on Vilene and stitch the shapes. Cut them out, making sure that the Vilene doesn't show. Place on water-soluble fabric and join the shapes using free-form machine stitching or built-in stitch patterns.

Above left: Arranged pieces on distressed velvet background, partly painted with spirit-soluble dyes.

Above right: The previous pieces of metal have been machine embroidered to the background. This left them looking rather stark. Integration was needed so a piece of chiffon was laid over the whole thing, stitched then zapped with a heat tool.

Metal with water-soluble paper

Water-soluble (dissolvable) paper can be tricky to work with but has such possibilities that it is worth making an effort to master it. In particular, it can be used with metal shim to give the effect of rusting, degraded artifacts and it is possible to make lighter, lacier edgings with the paper.

It works like this:

Carved Bark: 12 x 7 in (30 x 18 cm). A heavily embossed piece of metal is the focal point for this work. This was applied to painted, tissued Vilene and then areas of the Vilene were cut away. Pieces of water-soluble fabric were stitched over the cutouts. Shim was then stitched to the edges of the Vilene and embossed before being colored with waxes and Pearl Ex powders. Finally, an interesting shape was achieved by bending the metal edges.

1 Color the metal with heat and draw lines with the embossing tool, if required. Place the metal on craft Vilene cut to the same size. Using the water-soluble paper double, cut into strips to be placed over the metal; top and bottom gives good edges. Brush out some puff paint (Xpandaprint) onto glass or plastic and use a stamp or block to decorate some areas of the paper. *Do not heat the paint yet.* Then lay the paper over the metal shim so that it overlaps the edge.

2 Use free running stitch to attach the paper to the metal. This stitching will not show too much in the final piece. Change the foot and work some random built-in patterns. They should look like part of an old design that has become eroded. After stitching use a heat tool or an iron to puff the paint.

3 Now use nail polish or Pebeo (Crystal) Gel as a resist on some areas of the water-soluble paper. Don't use too much—the effect you want is a lacy, fragmented, distressed effect on the metal. You can see where it is used in the photo below.

4 When the nail polish or Pebeo Gel is dry, pin it all to a sheet of polystyrene foam and very, very carefully, with a paintbrush, add water. Just have a bowl of cold water on hand and splash with your paintbrush. You will find that areas of the paper that aren't resisted will turn into soggy mounds. This is to be encouraged. Move the soggy mounds around with the brush, especially over the metal. Make sure that the edges are particularly light and delicate.

5 When you have finished this, dab it very gently with a paper towel and then allow it to dry. It needs to be completely dry. When it is, paint it, either with a metal paint or with an acrylic.

6 When the painting is finished and dry, apply metallic wax and luster powders to both surfaces so that you have integrated them to look like the same piece of work. Any of the finishes in Chapter 6 will work. If you have used metal paints, the patination fluids, including rust, can be used. Spirit-soluble dyes look great, too. You should have an effect similar to that in the photo below.

Water-soluble paper can be an interesting surface when placed on the metal. The steps are shown here. First the paper was stamped with Xpandaprint and lightly stitched. The paper was then heated so that the Xpandaprint puffed. The next step was to apply a resist—in this case nail polish. Then, water was very gently splashed on, to dissolve the paper. Not all the paper was dissolved. As you can see, this stage looks a bit messy but the last two stages show the effect of painting and waxing this surface.

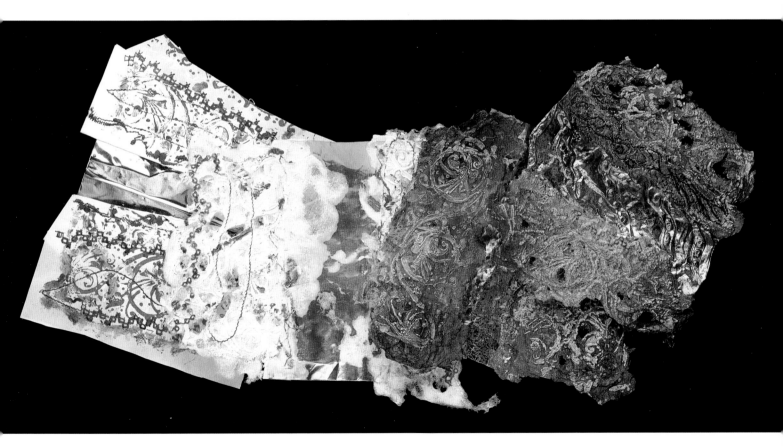

Metal Flora: 12 x 7 in (30 x 18 cm). Embroidery with water-soluble paper. The method shown in the previous photograph has been employed here. You can see how exciting the gleam of the metal is when it comes through the paper. The stitching is just visible in this piece of work.

Applying fabrics to metal

Interesting effects can be obtained by stitching fabric onto the metal, rather than the other way around. This is even more interesting if the metal is stitched first. Start by taking some colored metal shim. Use any of the ideas in Chapter 6. Place on craft Vilene and work bands of stitching. Then try placing strips of fabric, or stitched water-soluble paper, over the top and using free running stitch to secure and add texture. Work small samples to get the feel of the technique.

Here are some ideas.

- Bond sheer fabric to metal and then zap with a heat tool. Try stitching the fabric first.
- Stitch some Kunin (acrylic felt) to the metal. Zap with a heat tool after stitching. This looks good when cut into shapes, too.
- Cut up some space-dyed velvet—the fine, acrylic variety. Place strips on the metal and stitch. Use free running stitch and work in small circles to make the most of the texture.

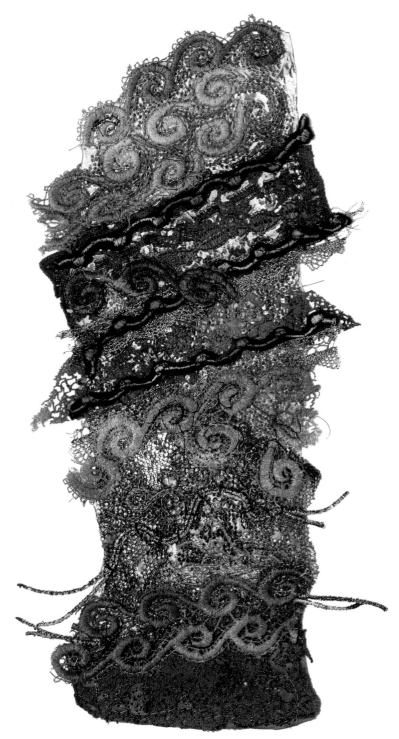

Gilded Lace: 15 x 36 cm (6 x 14 in). Here metal forms an underlying base for a series of applied fabrics. Painted lace motifs, cutout pieces of built-in patterns and nets, with some embossing powder applied to them, were all stitched onto the metal in this embroidery. The metal gleams through but the shine was knocked back. Machine-wrapped cords made a finishing touch.

A piece of water-soluble fabric over metal is used for this book cover. The fabric was designed and stitched first, then laid over the shim. Embossing tools were used to draw a pattern around the edges and into the gaps in the water-soluble piece of stitching. After stitching the water-soluble piece, the metal was colored using acrylic paints. The spine shows braids stitched, with strips of metal cut out with a paper punch.

- Apply scraps of painted lace. Stitch them to the metal, working around the pattern on the lace. Brush on some Pebeo (Crystal) Gel paint and sprinkle with embossing powder. Heat until it bubbles. If you have a purpose-made Melting-Pot (see page 112), melt the thick embossing powder in that and pour it over the lace.
- Stitch built-in patterns or heavy machine embroidery on felt or painted craft Vilene. Cut it out close to the stitching and then place on the metal and stitch around the edge to integrate it.
- Make some embossed fragments from paper pulp as described on page 24. Paint these and apply to the metal with lots of stitching to blend in.
- Try free-form machine stitching a design on water-soluble fabric. Make sure you lock the stitches by working several lines of stitch over each other. Dissolve the fabric and apply to previously embossed and color-heated metal. Apply the water-soluble fragment by hand or machine.

Borders

Metal is particularly effective for making borders. For inspiration, look at the wonderful illuminated manuscripts such as the *Lindisfarne Gospels* or the *Book of Kells*. Some of the pages are almost entirely composed of borders, interspersed with roundels or motifs. The borders described here can be used with an embossed center or a Lazertran image as the main center of interest. They could also be used with the patches described in the next section.

A good technique that you might try is to work strips of built-in machine stitches using a variegated thread on the metal shim or Wiremesh, which could be colored with heat before making the border. Make sure that the thread you choose has good color contrasts as these will show up as you stitch. It is easier to stitch the strips on a larger piece of Vilene and cut them out after stitching. Work as follows.

This drawing is based on one of the wonderful pages in the *Book of Kells*. You will note how this is composed of long borders and other areas that could be patches. On page 115, you can see a partly stitched version of this design.

Here are some samples that could be made into borders. The strips of metal or Wiremesh have been heavily stitched with built-in patterns using variegated threads. The thread used was wound on a card and is shown with its relevant strip so that you can see how the colors work. The strip at the bottom was stitched on Wiremesh, which was later burned to give an ancient and tatty look. These would just need edging to make wonderful borders.

1 Cut a piece of heavy Vilene (interfacing) about 6 x 8 in (15 x 20 cm).

2 Cut out a piece of black fabric such as cotton or polycotton and lay it over the Vilene before stitching. Place strips of metal about 1 in (2.5 cm) across on top of this. The black fabric will stop the holes in the metal made by the needle from showing white. It also gives a more dramatic effect.

3 Now machine stitch across the band of metal with a variegated thread using a built-in stitch pattern. The stitches can follow a pattern or form random lines. Remember the difference that stitch direction and thread color can make. In the photo below the thread is shown alongside each piece, so you can get an idea of the way the color changes.

These pieces make wonderful borders and, as you can see, the stitching is knocking-back the shine. If you are feeling brave, try stitching on Wiremesh and burning the stitching with a candle. Do this outside with a bowl of water handy and put out any flames by covering immediately with a heavy, damp cloth or dunking in the bucket. When dry, iron interfacing on the back to prevent the stitching from unravelling.

An alternative to the metal border is to use the tissue/Vilene background (see page 102) with metal cutouts free-form machine stitched along the length. Or use this background with metallic embossing powder and a rubber stamp with an intricate design for an all-over border pattern.

Both types of border benefit from applied wire shapes, perhaps with beads. The borders can be used as long strips or cut into sections. The next step is to edge the strips.

A variety of borders are shown here with wire, small pieces of metal, cutout stitching and frayed cable wires applied to them. Note how the borders have been edged. Buttonhole stitch, dimension paint, embossing powders, and cut strips of Vilene (interfacing) were all used.

Border edges

The edges of the borders will probably need to be finished in some way. There are several methods for doing this.

- Cut strips of tea-dyed craft Vilene (interfacing) to make a narrow border all around the metal strip. Put in place and stitch down using a narrow built-in stitch pattern.
- Embossing powder could be used. Just paint the edges of the strip with Pebeo Gel and dip them into some powder shaken onto a sheet of paper. When well coated, heat them with a heat tool to puff them up. An alternative to this method is to purchase a Melting-Pot, a wonderful invention that heats and melts embossing powder. When the powder is melted, the border or tile can be dipped into the pot, using tongs or tweezers.
- Dimensional paint can make neat edges. Just pipe the paint along the edge of the border and place on baking parchment to set.
- Wrap pipe cleaners with textured yarn and bend them around the edge. Couch them down by hand. Fancy stitches could be used here.
- Buttonhole stitches could be worked by hand around the edge.

Patches

Patches are small pieces of embroidery. They can be applied as design elements in a variety of shapes to enhance a focal point. In some cases a large patch could form the focal point.

Some of the design ideas for making patches. You will have plenty of ideas of your own for these.

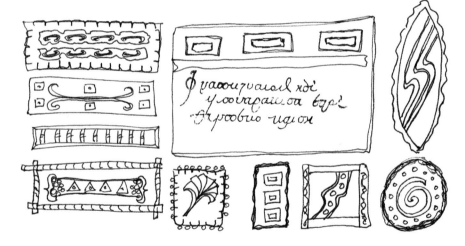

A good background to make patches is tissue paper bonded to felt or craft Vilene to make a fabric. This is then either tea-dyed or painted and a little metallic wax is used to add a gleam. This base is cut up into the appropriate shapes and further fabrics or metals applied to it. These could include some of the following.

Right: Samples of patches are shown here. There are many different ways of making these patches. Most of these show a base of tissue paper on Vilene (interfacing), suitably cutout. Small pieces of Xpandaprint were painted and applied, and some metal and wires were also used.

- Black Xpandaprint or puff paint can make interesting small tiles to stitch onto a patch. The paint can be placed in a squeeze container with a nozzle that gives thin lines of piping. These are often used for gutta with silk paint. Pipe out some shapes, like the ones shown in the diagram overleaf, onto craft Vilene (interfacing). Then scatter some embossing powder over the top (there are some available that look very antique), shake off the excess and puff the paint. Take care not to burn the interfacing. Paint with any permanent medium—silk paints or acrylics—and cut out the individual pieces to stitch onto the patches.

This is one of the components of patches that can be very useful. Black Xpandaprint is placed in a bottle with a nozzle and then piped into shapes on interfacing. Another way to do this is to use a cocktail stick, dip it into the Xpandaprint and use that for making the longer lines. The shapes were painted after puffing.

Small designs like these work well to make the Xpandaprint pieces ready to apply.

- Strips of metal or Wiremesh could be cut and stitched to the patch.
- Rubber-stamped images could be used, either on their own or with embossing powder.
- Small pieces of metal could be shaped in the paper crinkler and applied.
- Little tiles could be made of embossed metal, used plain, or colored by any of the methods described in Chapter 6.
- Heavier metal could be applied, such as domes or curled strips.
- The Melting-Pot can be used to great effect. Small pieces of net or lace could be dipped into it and stitched to the patch. Better still, try small pieces of embroidery —a good use for a piece of work that went wrong. Or the embossing powder could be drizzled from the Melting-Pot onto the patch and beads set into it. There are so many opportunities with this gadget.

There are, of course, many more ways of stitching the metal and you will be sure to have some ideas of your own. In Chapter 8 we consider ways of putting all these stitch techniques together to make completed textiles.

This shows the *Kells* design from page 109 partly stitched. You can see some of the borders and patches already stitched in place. The paper design was cut out and placed on a dark fabric to give ideas of where the next pieces will go. You will find that the design changes as you stitch, but it is a good idea to make a pattern to give yourself an initial idea for the placement and to see how the shapes work together.

8
Putting it All Together

We have looked at different ways of inscribing, decorating, coloring, and stitching metal and you probably have some plans of your own for combining all the elements in your textiles. Some ideas are described here, but don't feel you have to copy them—use them as a base from which to launch your own work. Using a variety of borders and patches will help to combine the techniques.

Icons and manuscripts

Tremendous inspiration can be gained from illuminated manuscripts or some of the wonderful historic icons. These lend themselves in particular to the metal treatment, especially when Lazertran is brought in for the main images. Try to trace, copy, or draw and paint the design yourself as there may be copyright issues in photocopying from a book. Emphasize the outlines before copying onto the Lazertran as they may fade a little in the transfer. The following is the method of construction.

First make a background—this method is suitable for both icons and manuscripts.

1 Cut a piece of craft Vilene to the size required and then cut a piece of Wonder Under (fusible webbing) to that size and a piece of tissue paper slightly larger. If you have a computer and inkjet printer, you may want to print onto the tissue paper before using it, especially with manuscripts where you might use a word processor to type random words or phrases to be printed on your tissue paper. The way to do this is as follows.

    a Cut a piece of tissue paper to 8½ x 11 in (21.6 x 27.9 cm) or A4 size and then apply a gluestick firmly around the edges of a piece of ordinary A4 printing paper, photocopy paper, or whatever you use in your printer.

    b Press the tissue onto the glued paper, making sure that all the edges are covered with tissue paper and very firmly stuck. This should go through an inkjet printer without any problem. (It is not advisable to use this method on a laser printer.)

    c Put this sheet through the printer to get your words onto it and then release the tissue paper by cutting or pulling it away from the glued edges.

If you don't have access to a computer, find a rubber stamp with lettering. Stamp with black or brown ink and try for a distressed look. Or, try copying some manuscript-type writing or calligraphy. Whichever method you use, allow the paper to dry overnight. You are now ready for the second step.

2 Crumple the tissue gently, then iron the Wonder Under onto the craft Vilene (interfacing), making sure it is very well stuck. Now pull the paper from the Wonder Under. While the Wonder Under is still warm, put your crumpled tissue paper on top of it, adding a few extra crumples as you lay it down. When you are satisfied, iron it well again through waxed paper.

Flat Plan for a Landscape:
12 x 24 in (30 x 60 cm). The idea
for this embroidery was based on
the page plans used by editors
and writers, which are usually
bristling with Post-it notes. I had an
idea that God's page plan might
look a little like this. The center is a
tissue-paper design with raised
areas of Lazertranned metal. This
represents the boiling earth. The
little notes around the edges are all
patches, which say things like "No
Fishing" and "Grass and Trees Go
Here."

You can see here an icon piece under construction. Stitching has begun on the metal that was Lazertranned with an angel design from a sketch book. In this case, the lettering was drawn (and smudged) directly onto a tea-dyed and webbing-sprayed background.

3   You can now dab the tissue paper with teabags. Tea-dyeing gives a very satisfying aged-manuscript look to a piece. Pour a very little amount of boiling water over the teabags. This can be adjusted to get the color you require. If you want to add more color, you can put a spot or two of silk paint onto your teabag and use that while dabbing. Use it sparingly though; you don't want large areas of color. The background should be quite neutral on these pieces.

4 Now let the background dry completely. To distress the lettering, stitch over a piece of tea-dyed diaper liner, fine agricultural fleece, Sizoflor, or Thermogauze vanishing muslin. Rub with a Shiva (Markal) oilstick and zap with a heat tool. Finally, rub on a very little wax, which can be Liberon or Treasure Gold. Rub very, very lightly, just highlighting a few creases. You may wish, before applying the wax, to add a squirt of black webbing spray (Krylon), which gives a darker look. Sometimes these pieces with the tea-dye can be too similar in color, so a little bit of the dark webbing spray works wonders—but make sure you spray *before* you apply the wax, or it won't stick.

This shows three ways of distressing stamped, lettered backgrounds to give an aged look. The top is Thermogauze, the middle is diaper liner and the bottom shows Sizoflor—all zapped after stitching.

You now have a background ready for you to make up into either a manuscript piece or an icon. We will look at the icon piece first.

1 From your sketchbook, choose a suitable icon image and copy it onto Lazertran. Float it off the Lazertran, as described on page 95, and put it onto the metal. When completely dry, heat with a heat tool to merge the Lazertran image completely with the metal.

2 Now place the image in a suitable position on your background. This will obviously be the focal point of the work. Look at books containing images of icons; they will give you lots of ideas. It really is worth spending a little time on the design of these pieces. Just sketch out some rough elements of the design first; then you won't be working completely in the dark.

3 When you are happy with the placement of the metal on the background, it's time to begin stitching. Using one of the temporary adhesives will help to hold the metal in place. Use stitch or embossing powders on the image and then wax on top of that to knock back the shine.

4 When you have done that, consider how you might make borders around this particular part of the design. Perhaps stitch some built-in patterns onto black felt, cut them out and stitch them over the top of the metalled image. When you are completely happy with this part of the design, move onto other design elements. Some of the shaped patches would work well.

5 You will have prepared these patches in advance. Consider that they might be shapes cut out in metal and perhaps stitched onto another piece of tissue bonded to craft Vilene (or interfacing), and free-form machine stitched. Or they could be strips of such designs with borders made from built-in stitch patterns. Consider all these elements first.

6 Other things that work well can be to added to the design. These could include raised domes or some of the heavy metal strips curled into shapes. Use free running stitch to attach the patches to the background.

7 When your icon piece is complete, consider how you might frame it. They can be most effective framed straight onto a piece of medium-density fiberboard (MDF). The embroidery can be firmly glued to the fiberboard with contact adhesive and the edges of the board could have strips of tea-dyed tissue on Vilene glued to them. With care, it is possible to oversew or buttonhole the edges.

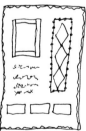

Manuscript pieces can be worked in much the same way. Have a look at some of the Celtic or Anglo-Saxon manuscripts, and try taking a single element, exaggerating the size and working into it with stitching and then framing it with lots of little border pieces. If you look at something like the *Lindisfarne Gospels*, you will find that they are incredibly well constructed with design elements placed in long borders.

These pieces can be constructed in exactly the same way as the icon pieces.

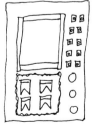

Designs for icon embroidery.

Alternatives for patches

Sometimes just one large patch works well (see below). Alternatively, find ways of integrating a tissue print with Lazertran on metal. A computer design could be used and printed on tissue as described on page 116, or the tissue could be painted, inked, and bleached, or otherwise decorated. An abstract design is best. Here is the method.

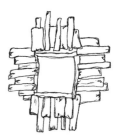

1 Bond colorful decorated tissue to Vilene (interfacing). Paint and wax, if necessary.

2 Take this piece to the copy shop and have the design photocopied onto Lazertran. Float the Lazertran onto metal and heat it to transfer the toner.

3 Cut the colored metal into shapes that will fit well with the design. Move them around to get the best design. If you want the metal to be slightly raised then back the cutout shapes with felt.

4 Stitch the metal to the tissue piece. If using felt, stitch around the shape and then cut away the excess. Stitch the edges again to integrate (see the effect on page 117).

5 Make patches to enhance the design. These could be placed around the edges as a border or become an integral part of the design. Attach by hand or with free running stitch. The diagrams (right) show some ideas.

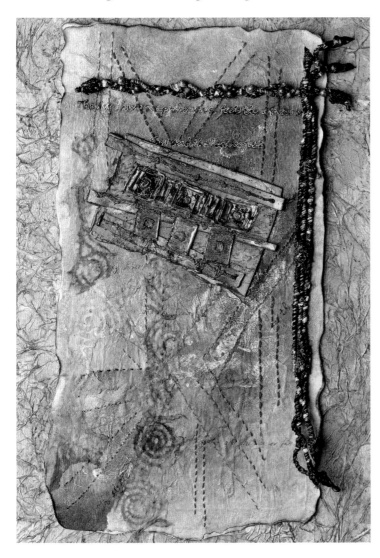

The Sky Shivers: 12 x 20 in (30 x 50 cm). Tissue paper on Vilene was painted and then lines from a poem about winter were written by hand. A large patch with metal and Xpandaprint pieces was applied together with pieces of Japanese paper, painted and waxed.

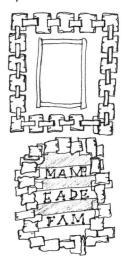

Right: Ideas for using patches as frames.

Weaving techniques with paper and metal

Metal can work very well combined with strips of stitched paper to give a woven effect. Shaped pieces of metal could form a central point or be placed to one side. The metal will probably form the center of interest so be aware of this when planning your squares.

Metallic Weave: 12 x 12 in (30 x 30 cm). This shows a woven embroidery using the paper-strip method with stamped images. The strips were colored with inks and decorated with foil. Note the heavily embossed squares of metal that lift and enhance the design.

Opposite: *Knight and his Lady* (height 16 in/40 cm). These delightful figures were made by Chris Hardy using the paper-weaving method. She varied the size of the strips to make them thinner for the limbs and larger for the body. They have faces and hearts made from embossed metal.

First of all, emboss your metal and color it as you wish. A small motif is ideal for this. The shapes could be squares, triangles, or rectangles—these particular shapes seem to work better for this technique than amorphous shapes. The metal can be colored in any way you choose, but obviously the color of the strips will influence this.

Now for the woven strips. It is possible to use fabric, but paper is especially easy to work with because you don't have to worry about the edges. If you use a fabric, you must finish the edges in some way. Burning, overstitching, or something similar, or using a product like Fray Check, will stop the edges wearing away. Be aware when weaving strips that the edges rub together, so it needs to be a fairly permanent solution.

You could try handmade paper, painted in bright colors. Stamp over the top with rubber stamps or Rollagraphs (these are stamps on a roller which work really well here). Use clear embossing fluid and clear powder. Heat with a heat tool. Now iron some transfer foil over the top. Try to use an old piece of foil so that the metallic effect is not too heavy. Then paint with black or colored ink. The embossing powder will resist the ink and allow the color underneath to show through. If you use a bleach-reactive ink then try bleaching on top for extra interest. Cut into strips of suitable size. Stitch if required. Built-in stitch patterns work well. Stitch onto black felt to thicken the strips. Trim the felt close to the edges.

When you have done all this and prepared your strips and your metal pieces, cut a piece of Vilene (interfacing) to the size of the finished piece. You may be making a piece to stand in its own right, or maybe a 'quilt' where you piece all your weavings together afterwards. Whichever technique you use, you will need to cut the interfacing to size.

Use your strips to build up the shape. This could be traditional weaving with the strips running in and out of each other and the metal placed as required, or perhaps a log-cabin effect around the piece of metal. Whichever you want to do, make sure that the strips surround the metal and are firmly held together. Pin them firmly to the interfacing to hold in place as you weave.

Then try some stitching. This could be almost invisible, with just stab stitching from the back to hold the strips down, or quite heavy machine embroidery that could be worked over the weaving to hold it in place. Fold the ends of the strips over to the back and secure to finish.

As you can see, there are many ways of combining the metal with paper, fabric, wire, and other media. Do give them all a try, carry out lots of experiments—and have fun along the way.

Opposite: A delicate embroidery 6 x 8 in (15 x 20 cm) by Sue Miles using metal and paper strips woven with razor shells. The shells were stamped with lettering and the base is tea-dyed tissue and Vilene. The colors are sympathetic to the shells and enhance them.

Below: Ready-to-weave strips.

Resources and Bibliography

Sewing machines

Bernina of America
3702 Prairie Lake Ct.
Aurora, IL 60504
(630) 978-2500
www.berninausa.com

Brother Home Sewing & Embroidery Sales
777 North Brother Blvd.
Bartlett, TN 38133
(901) 379-1010
www.brothersews.com

Janome America, Inc.
10 Industrial Ave.
Mahwah, NJ 07430
(201) 825-3200
www.janome.com

VSM Sewing, Inc.
31000 Viking Pkwy.
Westlake, OH 44145
(440) 808-6550
(800) 446-2333
www.husqvarnaviking.com
www.whitesewing.com
www.pfaffusa.com
(Husqvarna Viking, Pfaff, and White sewing machines)

Singer Sewing Company
1224 Heil Quaker Blvd.
PO Box 7017
LaVergne, TN 37086
(800) 474-6437
www.singerco.com

General supplies

Glass paint, paper cutters, wood and leather dyes, Polymer clay, and Pebeo Gel are available from art and hobby stores and from onlines sources. Wonder Under is available from fabric stores. You can buy embossing powders from stamp shops. Finishing waxes and wood dyes may be purchased at lumber yards or home supply and hardware stores. Contact fine cabinet and musical instrument makers for local sources of wood dyes and finishing products.

Equipment and materials

The ABoyd Company
PO Box 4568
Jackson, MS 39296
(888) 458-2693
International customers call:
(601) 948-3477
www.aboyd.com
(Friendly Plastic)

American Art Clay Co., Inc.
Brent Pottery Equipment
Genesis Artist Colors International
6060 Guion Rd.
Indianapolis, IN 46254-1222
(800) 374-1600
(317) 244-6871
www.amaco.com
(art and hobby supplies, modeling clays, metal sheets, Wireform, Wiremesh)

ArtCity.com
1011 W. 190th St.
Gardena, CA 90248
(866) 278-2489
(310) 630-0071
www.artcity.com
(Lazertran papers)

Carriage House Paper
79 Guernsey St.
Brooklyn, NY 11222
(800) 669-8781
www.carriagehousepaper.com
(papermaking supplies)

Clearsnap, Inc.
PO Box 98
Anacortes, WA 98221
(888) 448-4862
www.clearsnap.com
(molding mats, Rollagraphs)

Craft Supplies USA
PO Box 50300
Provo, UT 84605
(800) 551-8876
www.woodturnerscatalog.com
(Liberon products)

Embroidery Adventures
PO Box 40504
Bellevue, WA 98015
(866) 270-9390
www.embroideryadventures.com
store.embroideryadventures.com
(embroidery supplies)

Fabrics to Dye For
67 Tom Harvey Rd.
Westerly, RI 02891
(888) 322-1319
(401) 348-0779
www.fabricstodyefor.com
(Pebeo Tagger paint)

Gerber Parent Resource Center
445 State St.
Fremont, MI 49413
(800) 443-7237
www.gerber.com
(diaper liners)

Golden Artist Colors, Inc.
188 Bell Rd.
New Berlin, NY 13411-9527
(607) 847-6154
(800) 959-6543
www.goldenpaints.com
(interference colors)

Impress Me
17116 Escalon Dr.
Encino, CA 91436-4030
(818) 788-6730
www.impressmenow.com
(stamping supplies)

Kunin Felt, Foss Manufacturing Company, Inc.
380 Lafayette Rd.
PO Box 5000
Hampton, NH 03843-5000
(603) 929-6100
www.kuninfelt.com
(zappable felt)

Lazertran LLC
5535A NW 35th Ave.
Fort Lauderdale, FL 33309
(800) 245-7547
www.lazertran.com
(laser transfer papers)

Luthiers Mercantile International, Inc.
7975 Cameron Dr. Bldg. 1600
Windsor, CA 95492
(707) 687-2020
(800) 477-4437
www.lmii.com
(spirit-soluble dyes, denatured alcohol)

Meinke Toy
#411
55 E. Long Lake Rd.
Troy, MI 48085
(248) 813-9806
meinketoy.com
(Bondaweb, vanishing muslin, Grilon, Vilene, other UK surface products)

Paper Direct
1025 E. Woodman Rd.
Colorado Springs, CO 80920
(800) 272-7377
For international orders (outside 48 contiguous U.S., Canada, or U.S. territories):
www.paperdirect.com
(color foil, transfer papers)

Polymer Clay Express at TheArtWay Store
9890 Main St.
Damascus, MD 20872
(301) 482-0399
(800) 844-0138
www.polymerclayexpress.com
(art and hobby supplies, Melting Pots)

Sepp Leaf Products, Inc.
381 Park Ave. S.
New York, NY 10016
(212) 683-2840
(800) 971-7377
www.seppleaf.com
www.liberon.com (France)
(U.S. importer for Liberon products)

Wet Paint, Inc.
1684 Grand Ave.
St. Paul, MN 55105
(651) 698-6431
www.wetpaintart.com
(art supplies, Pebeo Crystal Gel)

Wood Finishing Supplies
855 38th St.
Rochester, MN 55901
(866) 548-1677
(507) 280-6515
www.woodfinishingsupplies.com
(spirit-soluble dyes and stains, Liberon products)

www.quiltingarts.com
(online store; surface design supplies, vanishing muslin)

Bibliography

Campbell-Harding, Valerie. *Machine Embroidery Stitch Techniques*. London: Batsford, 2003.

Dawson, Sophie. *The Art and Craft of Papermaking*. Asheville, North Carolina: Lark Books, 1997.

Kieffer, Suzan Mowery, ed. *Fiberarts Design Book 7*. Loveland, Colorado: Interweave Press, 2004.

Stearns, Lynn, ed. *Papermaking for Basketry and Other Crafts*. Asheville, North Carolina: Lark Books, 1992.

Thackeray, Beata. *Paper-Making-Decorating-Designing*. New York: Watson-Guptill, 1998.

Index